# LIFE IN THE UNITED KINGDOM

Home Office   A Journey to Citizenship

The official publication valid for tests taken from April 2007

For information on Life in the UK tests, visit www.lifeintheuktest.gov.uk

Large Print Version

**TSO**
information & publishing solutions

Published by TSO (The Stationery Office) and available from:

| | |
|---|---|
| **Online** | www.tsoshop.co.uk |

**Mail,Telephone, Fax & E-mail**
TSO
PO Box 29
Norwich NR3 1GN

**Telephone orders/General enquiries:** 0870 600 5522
**Fax orders:** 0870 600 5533
**E-mail:** customer.services@tso.co.uk

**Textphone** 0870 240 3701

**TSO Shops**
16 Arthur Street
Belfast BT1 4GD

**Textphone** 028 9023 8451
**Fax** 028 9023 5401

71 Lothian Road
Edinburgh EH3 9AZ

**Textphone** 0870 606 5566
**Fax** 0870 606 5588

TSO@Blackwell and other Accredited Agents

Published with the permission of the Home Office on behalf of Her Majesty's Stationery Office.

Second edition. Fourth impression February 2010

This publication has been approved by Ministers and has official status.

Applications for reproduction should be made to:

**The Licensing Division**
Office of Public Sector Information
St Clements House
1-16 Colegate
Norwich
NR3 1BQ

Fax 01603 723000 or e-mail:
licensing@cabinet-office.x.gsi.gov.uk

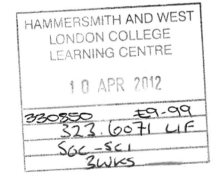

# FOREWORD

The Home Secretary
The Rt Hon
John Reid MP

The first edition of this handbook became a best-seller when it came out towards the end of 2004. Some people will have bought it out of interest, or a wish to know more about the United Kingdom's history and institutions. And many more will have obtained it as a study guide for the new tests of knowledge about life in the United Kingdom which we brought in during 2005 for people who want to become British citizens.

Those tests, together with the new citizenship ceremonies which celebrate the achievement of new Britons in becoming citizens, have been a real success. They have encouraged people who have decided to make their lives in Britain to learn more about our culture and institutions, and in many cases to improve their knowledge of our language. We think that the benefits of this approach in creating strong and cohesive communities are clear. That is why, from 2 April 2007, we will also be asking people who apply for permanent settlement in the United Kingdom – which must be obtained before someone can apply for citizenship – to pass the same test.

We have taken the opportunity to revise this handbook thoroughly. I would like to thank heartily the members of the Advisory Board on Naturalisation and Integration who have led this task. We have taken account of the many comments made about the handbook.

Whether you are reading this handbook in order to take the settlement test, or simply to increase your knowledge of British life and institutions, I hope that, like many thousands of others, you will find it both interesting and helpful.

## How to use this handbook

This handbook is intended for those readers who are intending to become permanent residents or citizens of the United Kingdom, and are studying it in order to take the tests of knowledge of English and of life in the United Kingdom which all applicants now need to pass.

Since 2005, everyone who applies to become a British citizen has had to show their knowledge of the English language and of life in the United Kingdom in one of two ways. They can take a special ESOL (English for Speakers of Other Languages) course, which uses teaching materials based on the practical meaning of citizenship. Or they can take the new Life in the UK test, which consists of 24 questions about important aspects of life in Britain today. Those 24 questions will be different for each person taking the test. The Life in the UK Test will normally be taken in English, although special arrangements can be made if anyone wishes to take it in Welsh or Scottish Gaelic. The questions are deliberately written in a way that requires an understanding of the English language at the level (called ESOL Entry 3 level) that the law requires of people becoming British citizens. So there is no need to take a separate test of knowledge of the English language.

From 2 April 2007, everyone who applies for permanent residence in the United Kingdom (often called 'settlement' or 'indefinite leave to remain') will also need to qualify either by taking the special ESOL course or by passing the Life in the UK test. A person who qualifies for settlement

in either of these ways will not need to go through the same process again if he or she later decides to apply for British citizenship. This handbook contains all the answers to the questions that may be asked in the Life in the UK test. The questions will all be based on chapters 2, 3, 4, 5 and 6 of the handbook. You do not have to study the other chapters in order to be able to pass the test, but we hope and believe that they will be of interest and practical value to many readers and they will certainly help your understanding of the chapters you will be tested on. The handbook has been written to ensure that anyone who can read English at the ESOL Entry 3 level or above should have no difficulty with the language.

To provide extra help for readers who are not native English speakers, we have provided at the end of the handbook a glossary of some key words and phrases, which you may find helpful. We have also highlighted some areas that are particularly important. These are headed 'Make sure you understand' but are intended only as guidance; reading just these sections will not be enough to pass the test. You may not get questions on these highlighted areas, and you may be asked about topics that have not been highlighted. So please make sure you read each chapter carefully.

We would also advise you to think carefully before purchasing any of the 'study guides' to the Life in the UK test which can sometimes be found in bookshops or on the internet. None of these is officially approved, even though some suggest they are, and may not be of much help to you. Some might even mislead you by suggesting you memorise answers to questions that aren't genuine and are very different to the ones you will be asked in your test.

If you want to find out more information about the Life in the UK test, please visit the website of UFI, the company that manages them on behalf of the Home Office. This website (www.lifeintheuktest.gov.uk) gives contact details for centres where the test can be taken, background information about the tests and the fees involved, and also offers a sample test to give you an idea of what to expect. If you want information about the alternative way of obtaining permanent residence by taking a special ESOL with citizenship course, the UFI helpline on 0800 0154245, and your local library, are good sources of information on colleges offering these courses in your area.

The Government welcomes new migrants to Britain. We very much hope that those who meet our residence qualifications and decide to spend their lives in this country will seek permanent settlement, and will eventually go on to become British citizens. That is why we call our handbook 'A Journey to Citizenship'. We hope that this journey will be a fascinating and worthwhile one for you.

# CONTENTS

Chapter 1: THE MAKING OF THE
          UNITED KINGDOM

What's in a name?                        7
Early Britain                            8
The Middle Ages                         10
The early modern period                 13
Stability and the growth of empire      17
The 20th century                        23
Politics in Britain since 1945          25

Chapter 2: A CHANGING SOCIETY

Migration to Britain                    35
The changing role of women              37
Children, family and young people       38

Chapter 3: UK TODAY: A PROFILE

Population                              45
The nations and regions of the UK       48
Religion                                49
Customs and traditions                  51

Chapter 4: HOW THE UNITED
          KINGDOM IS GOVERNED

The British Constitution                55
The UK in Europe and the world          67

Chapter 5: EVERYDAY NEEDS

Housing                                 71
Services in and for the home            75
Money and credit                        78
Health                                  81
Education                               86
Leisure                                 91
Travel and transport                    93

Chapter 6: EMPLOYMENT

Looking for work                        99
Equal rights and discrimination        102
At work                                104
Working for yourself                   109
Childcare and children at work         111

Chapter 7: KNOWING THE LAW

The rights and duties of a citizen     115
Criminal courts                        119
Civil courts                           120
Legal advice and aid                   120
Human rights                           123
Children                               128
Consumer protection                    130

## Chapter 8: SOURCES OF HELP AND INFORMATION

Introduction                           135
Public libraries                       136
Citizens Advice Bureau                 137
The police service                     138
Other sources of information           139

## Chapter 9: BUILDING BETTER COMMUNITIES

Chapter 9: BUILDING BETTER            143
           COMMUNITIES
Cohesive communities                  **143**

# GLOSSARY

GLOSSARY                              153

# Chapter 1

# THE MAKING OF THE UNITED KINGDOM

To understand a country it is important to know something about its history. This section is a brief chronological account of how the United Kingdom came to be what it is today. Any account of history, however, is only one interpretation. Historians often disagree about what to include and what to exclude in historical accounts. As well as the main historical events and people, this section also mentions people who are not necessarily the most important historically, but whose names often appear in books, newspapers and on TV.

## What's in a name?

There is some confusion about the correct meanings and use of the terms 'United Kingdom', 'British Isles', 'Britain' and 'British'. The United Kingdom consists today of four countries: England, Scotland, Wales and Northern Ireland (the rest of Ireland is an independent country). These four countries came together at different times to form a union called the United Kingdom of Great Britain and Northern Ireland, which is the official name of the country. The name 'Britain' or 'Great Britain' refers only to England, Scotland and Wales, not to Northern Ireland. The adjective 'British', however, usually refers to everyone in the UK, including Northern Ireland. There are also several islands which are closely linked with the United Kingdom but do not form part of it: the Channel Islands and the Isle of Man. These have kept their own institutions of government and are called 'Crown Territories'.

In the United Kingdom, national identity and citizenship do not always mean the same thing. The Scottish and Welsh will usually say that they have British (or UK) citizenship, but that their nationality is Scottish or Welsh. In Northern Ireland some people say they are British, some people say they are Irish and some people say they are both. This depends on their political and cultural allegiances. People born in England will more often say that their nationality as well as their citizenship is British.

Many important institutions are common to England, Scotland, Wales and Northern Ireland, such as the laws and customs of the Constitution, the Crown as a symbol of unity, and parliamentary and representative government. But there are many important differences between England, Scotland, Wales and Northern Ireland. Scotland, Wales and Northern Ireland now have parliaments or assemblies of their own, with limited but significant powers.

## Early Britain

In sport there are four different football teams which play separately in international competitions, but there is only one Olympic team for the whole of the United Kingdom.

In addition to national diversity, there is a very long tradition of ethnic and religious diversity in the United Kingdom. This goes back to early history, as you will see in this chapter.

### The Roman Conquest

In very early history the land was populated by tribes who came to the British Isles from different parts of Europe. Stonehenge, the great prehistoric temple which still stands in what is now the English county of Wiltshire, is one of the great monuments of prehistoric Europe. In later centuries Britain was invaded by Celtic tribes who had a sophisticated culture and economy. The people spoke Celtic dialects which later became the languages which are spoken today in some parts of Wales, Scotland and Ireland.

### The Romans

In 55 BC the Romans, who had an empire covering most of the Mediterranean lands, first came to Britain with Julius Caesar. Nearly a hundred years later they came back and began a conquest of all of Britain except the highlands of Scotland. There was strong opposition from the native tribes who fought to try to keep the Romans out. A famous tribal leader who fought the Romans was Boudicca, the queen of the Iceni in what is now eastern England. Later, when the tribes in the south of the island had been conquered, one of the emperors, Hadrian, built a wall in the north of England to keep out the Picts (ancestors of the Scottish people; the Scots

were originally a tribe who came over from Ireland). Parts of this wall can still be seen today.

The Romans had a big impact on life in Britain. Before they left in 410 AD, they established medical practice, created a structure of administration and law, and built great public buildings and roads. The language of the Romans was Latin. Those local people who learned to speak, read and write Latin often became administrators and traders.

## After the Romans

As the Roman Empire gradually became weaker, new tribes invaded from northern Europe looking for better land. These were called the Jutes, Angles and Saxons. These people spoke dialects which later became the basis of English. The people of Britain fought against these new invaders and were led for a while in the 6th century by the legendary King Arthur. Eventually, however, the invaders took over all of southern and eastern Britain, setting up their own kingdoms and pushing the Britons to the west and to the north.

During the 6th century, missionaries from Rome led by St Augustine came to Britain and spread the new religion of Christianity across the south. Monks from Ireland did the same in the north of Britain.

## The Norse invaders

In the 8th and 9th centuries, Vikings from Denmark and Norway invaded Britain and Ireland. They conquered many of the small kingdoms of the east of England and Scotland. Gradually the kingdoms in England were united under the kings of Wessex and became strong enough to fight against the Vikings. King Alfred the Great defeated the Vikings in England at the end of the 9th century. They were also defeated in Scotland and Ireland. Yet many of the Viking invaders stayed, especially in the east of England where many names of places come from the Viking languages. They farmed the land, mixed with the local populations and converted to Christianity. For a while in the 11th century they again ruled England under King Canute. Their languages also had an influence on the early forms of English and, in Scotland, on Gaelic.

## The Norman Conquest

After King Canute, the Saxons again ruled England until an invasion led by William, Duke of Normandy (part of today's France) in 1066. He is also called William the Conqueror. William defeated Harold, the King of England, at the battle of Hastings. The Norman Conquest was the last successful foreign invasion of England.

The Normans took complete ownership of the

## The Middle Ages

### Times of war

land and introduced new laws and administration. Norman French became the official language and had a big influence on the Anglo-Saxon language of the common people. The Normans and the kings who followed them began the conquest of Wales and some parts of Ireland. They did not yet invade Scotland but the Scottish kings and nobility in the south were strongly influenced by Norman-French culture. The first Jewish settlements in the UK were also established at this time. William the Conqueror encouraged Jews from France to settle in Britain. Jewish communities grew up in several towns and cities.

The period after the Norman Conquest is called the Middle Ages or the medieval period. It lasted until about 1485. It was a time of almost constant war. In the 12th and 13th centuries, many knights from the British Isles took part in the Crusades, in which European Christians fought for control of Jerusalem and of other cities in the Holy Land. King Richard I (known as Richard the Lionheart) spent much of his reign taking part in the Crusades.

At home, the English kings tried to dominate the Welsh, the Scots and the Irish. The Scots, led by Robert the Bruce, defeated the English at the battle of Bannockburn in 1314; the

English kings were unable to conquer the Scots during the Middle Ages.

In Wales, however, the English managed to destroy the power of the Welsh princes by 1300. They built huge castles to maintain their power and by the middle of the 15th century the last Welsh rebellions had been put down. From 1536, England imposed its laws on Wales and the English language became compulsory for legal and official purposes.

During the Middle Ages, the English kings also fought a long war with the French, called the Hundred Years War. The English won some important battles against the French, such as the battle of Agincourt,

which Shakespeare describes in his play Henry V. Later the French fought back and reclaimed their country.

### The origins of Parliament

The origins of Parliament lie in the early Middle Ages. Before 1215, there were no laws to limit the power of the king of England. The most powerful landowners, the barons, wanted to make sure that their voices were heard and that new taxes could only be made with their agreement. In 1215, the barons forced King John to sign a charter of rights called the Magna Carta (which means the Great Charter). This was not a charter of rights for the common people, but it did take away the absolute

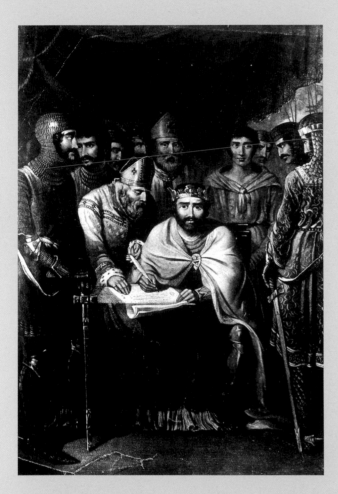

power of the king. The king could no longer collect taxes without the consent of the barons. To make or change laws he had to consult and negotiate with them. At the end of the 13th century, Parliament gradually became the place where the king consulted with his subjects.

The English Parliament was not unique: there were parliaments in Scotland and much of the rest of Europe in the Middle Ages.

The English Parliament did, however, become the most developed in Europe. The aristocrats and great landowners sat in the House of Lords, but there was also a separate House of Commons. The House of Commons represented country landowners and wealthy people in the market towns and cities. Judges began to develop English common law by a process of precedent and tradition. They were independent of the Crown. In Scotland there were similar developments, except that there were three Houses of Parliament (called 'estates'), the Lords, the Commons and the clergy, and the legal system developed as a codified one - the laws were written down.

In England, in Norman times, under the system called feudalism, landlords owned the land and the people who worked on their land were called serfs. They did not earn any money for their work on the land and were not allowed to move away, but they did have a small area of the lord's land on which they grew enough food to survive. The same system developed in southern Scotland, but in the north of Scotland and in Ireland land was owned in common by members of the 'clans'.

In 1348, a third of the population of England died in the plague called the Black Death. This was one of the worst disasters ever to strike Britain and Europe but because it created a shortage of labour it helped to improve conditions for the poor in the long run.

The feudal system gradually changed to a system based on wages. New social classes appeared, including large landowners called gentry and smaller farmers called yeomen.

They became much more independent of the great landlords than their ancestors had been. In the towns, growing wealth led to the development of a strong middle class by the end of the medieval period.

## The origins of the modern state

At the end of the Middle Ages, there was a 30-year civil war in England between two aristocratic groups, the supporters of the House (or family) of Lancaster and those of the House of York. This war was known as the Wars of the Roses, because the symbol of Lancaster was a red rose and the white rose was the symbol of York. In 1485 the civil war ended when Henry Tudor won the battle of Bosworth, killing Richard III. Henry became King Henry VII, and established the dynasty of the House of Tudor. Henry VII deliberately weakened the independent military power of the aristocracy and began to strengthen the central power of the state.

## Language, culture and immigration in the Middle Ages

During the Middle Ages an English language and culture gradually came into being. This was a mixture of Anglo-Saxon and Norman-French. Great cathedrals were built, many of them in use today. Three hundred years after the Norman Conquest, people in England began to think of themselves as one nation. One of the first works of literature to be written in English, a long poem called 'The Canterbury Tales' by Geoffrey Chaucer, was written at the end of the 14th century. It describes the many different kinds of people who met and went as pilgrims to a city called Canterbury. The poem is still popular today. In Scotland, the Middle Ages saw the development of the Scots language which was significantly different from the English spoken south of the Scottish border.

This period was also a time of trade. Merchants came from Germany and Italy. There were also people who came to England with special skills, such as weavers from France, engineers from Germany, glass manufacturers from Italy and canal builders from Holland. In 1440 there were 16,000 foreigners in England, approximately 1% of the population.

# The early modern period

## Religious conflicts

Henry VII had already begun to strengthen the central administration of England and reduce the military power of the aristocracy. His son Henry VIII continued this policy. Henry VIII was most famous for breaking away from the Church of Rome.

Henry VIII wanted a divorce because his wife, Catherine of Aragon, had not given him a surviving heir. In order to get a divorce and remarry he needed the approval of the Pope, who had authority over all Christians in western Europe. When the Pope refused, Henry established the Church of England. The king, not the Pope, now had the power to appoint the bishops and to decree what people were required to believe.

At the same time the Reformation - a great movement of opinion against the power of the Pope - was happening in England, Scotland, and many other European countries. The people who opposed the Pope were called Protestants. They read the Bible in their own languages instead of in Latin, and interpreted it for themselves. The Protestants believed that each individual's personal relationship with God was of supreme importance.The Catholics believed that it was essential to submit to the authority of the Church, as led by the Pope.

Protestant ideas gradually gained strength in England and Scotland during the 16th century, but were much less successful in Ireland.

In Ireland, the English attempted to impose Protestantism and English laws governing the inheritance of land. The leaders of the tribes in Ireland, the chieftains, rebelled against the English and there was much brutal fighting between the English and the Irish rebels. This created a sense of national consciousness which united Ireland. Many of the Norman-English who had settled in Ireland remained Catholic.

## The middle way: the reign of Elizabeth I

Henry VIII's only son and heir was Edward. Edward was strongly Protestant, but he died at the age of 15 and his half-sister Mary became queen. Mary was a devout Catholic and brought England back to obedience to the Pope. Under Mary, Protestants were persecuted. Mary, too, died after only a short reign and the next monarch was her half-sister, Elizabeth, a Protestant. Elizabeth I was more moderate than Mary in her religion. She re-established the Church of England and the Christian religion as practised in England became known as Anglicanism. Elizabeth expected everyone to attend church but did not ask questions about their real beliefs. By keeping to a 'middle way' between the Catholics and the more extreme Protestants (later called Puritans), Elizabeth managed to keep peace in England, despite her many enemies. Gradually, however, Elizabeth's popularity rose, along with strong feelings of English patriotism. These became stronger when the English defeated the attempt of the Spanish 'Armada' (or fleet) to conquer England and restore Catholicism in 1588.

In Scotland the Protestant reformation was more extreme and led to constant changes of government. 'Mary, Queen of Scots', was a cousin of Elizabeth I and was crowned queen of Scotland while she was only a baby. Her mother was French, so Mary was a Catholic. The rival groups in Scotland fought to control Mary. When her husband was murdered by her lover and her situation became more dangerous, Mary fled to England. Elizabeth I, however, believed Mary wanted to try to take over the English throne, and kept her in captivity for 20 years. Later Mary was executed, accused of plotting against Elizabeth I.

## Culture and discovery

Today the Elizabethan period is remembered for the richness of its poetry and drama, especially for the plays and poems of Shakespeare, who is still widely recognised as the greatest writer in English. The period is also important for England's discoveries and trade overseas, at a time when European countries began to exert power and influence in other parts of the world. Sir Francis Drake, commander in the defeat of the Spanish Armada, was one of the founders of England's naval tradition. In Elizabeth I's time, Englishsettlers first began to colonise the eastern coast of America, a movement which greatly increased in the next century.

## Two kingdoms, one king

When Elizabeth I died in 1603, she had no children. Her nearest relative was the king of Scotland, James VI. James was the son of Mary, Queen of Scots, but he was a Protestant. He became King James I of England but the two countries did not become united at this time. Scotland kept its own parliament for another hundred years and still has its own system of law.

## Ireland: rebellion and plantation

At this time, Ireland was an almost completely Catholic country. England had begun invasions into Ireland many centuries before (in the times of the Normans) but had only succeeded in occupying land around Dublin, an area called the 'Pale'. The Tudor kings Henry VII and Henry VIII had managed to gain control of the whole country and started to introduce English laws and to break down the power of the local leaders. During the rule of Elizabeth, rebellions against the English broke out, strengthened by the attempts of the English government to abolish the power of the Catholic Church. After one of these rebellions, James I began a policy of 'plantation' or colonisation by force in Ulster, the north-eastern province of Ireland. This involved replacing the Catholic landholders with English and especially Scottish Protestant farmers. Many 'planters' went to Ulster, mainly from the south-west of Scotland. Land taken from the Catholic rebels was given to companies in London. These events had serious long-term consequences for England, Scotland and Ireland.

## Charles I and Parliament

During the reigns of Elizabeth I and James I, the English Parliament became more powerful and influential. The king, Lords and Commons were supposed to be mutually dependent and respectful of each other, but there were strong merchant and commercial interests in the House of Commons, representing a growing middle class, many of whom wanted a more strongly Protestant policy.

Elizabeth I had many political skills and tried to balance these interests. James I and his son Charles I, however, were less skilled in managing these conflicts. Many thinkers in Europe at that time believed in the theory of 'the divine right of kings' - that the king was directly appointed by God. Charles I was particularly influenced by these ideas and, when he could not get Parliament to agree with his religious and foreign policies, he tried to rule without calling any more Parliaments. A number of refugees from the religious policies of James I and Charles I decided to settle in America, where they established the new Puritan colonies of New England.

Charles I tried to impose the ceremonies of the Church of England on the Protestants of Scotland, who were called Presbyterians. In response, the Scots invaded the north of England. Charles needed money to fight the Scots and this could only be granted by Parliament, but when it met in 1640, Parliament refused to vote to give money to the king to fight this war. Many in Parliament were Puritans who, like the Scots, opposed the king's religious policies; they saw no reason to help him suppress the Scots.

When the Catholics of Ireland, who were afraid that Parliament might attack their religion, rebelled in 1641,

Parliament demanded control of the army because they feared the king would use it against them. Charles I tried to arrest five parliamentary leaders, who fled. The chairman of the House of Commons (the Speaker) refused to tell the king where they had gone and said that he was loyal only to the command of the House of Commons. Civil war broke out in England in 1642.

## Oliver Cromwell and the English Republic

After four years Charles I was defeated by Parliament's general, the Puritan Oliver Cromwell. Charles, however, refused to compromise with Parliament and was executed in 1649. The Parliament itself had to submit to the rule of its own army and Members of Parliament who wanted peace with the king were expelled. For eleven years England became a republic for the only time in its history, under the leadership of Oliver Cromwell, who took the title of Lord Protector from 1653.

Many Scots had bitterly opposed the execution of Charles I, who was their king as well, and soon afterwards they crowned his son as King Charles II. Cromwell defeated Charles, in two battles at Dunbar and Worcester, and brought Scotland completely under his control. He also finally put down the Irish rebellion which had begun in 1641, using so much violence that even today the memory of Cromwell is still hated by some Irish Catholics.

Later, in the 19th century, the English came to see Cromwell as the defender of Parliament's rights against the Crown. When Cromwell died, however, there was no credible successor to his power and no clear system of government in place. The civil war had created religious and political extremism. Some groups of people questioned the whole foundation of the society and the ideas of property and social class. The first English democratic party, the Levellers, had briefly flourished in Parliament's armies but by the time of Cromwell's death most people were tired of change and wished for a return to stability.

## The Restoration

Parliament decided that the best solution was to bring back Charles II from his exile in the Netherlands. In 1660 he was recalled to England and crowned king. Charles II wanted power but he also understood that to rule in peace he could not repeat his father's mistakes. He was popular enough to get Parliament to support his policies and, though he was secretly a Catholic, he re-established the power of the Church of England. The Puritans who had ruled England and

### The Glorious Revolution

### Constitutional monarchy

Scotland during the Republic were kept out of power and treated harshly.

Charles had no legitimate children. When he died in 1685 his brother, James II, who was openly Catholic, became king. The Protestant majority in England rapidly became worried that he might wish to abolish the Church of England and force England back to obedience to the Pope. All James's actions during his short reign - his appointment of Catholics as army officers, his defiance of the laws made by Parliament and his quarrels with the bishops of the Church of England - made these suspicions stronger.

In 1688, the great lords who were opposed to James II conspired to ask William of Orange, the Protestant ruler of the Netherlands, to invade England and proclaim himself king. William was married to James II's daughter, Mary. When he invaded, there was no resistance in England, and he and Mary took over the throne. This change was later called the 'Glorious Revolution' in England because it was accomplished without bloodshed and because it ended the threat of arbitrary royal power.

James II still had many supporters, especially in Scotland and Ireland, who were called Jacobites.

James was determined to reclaim the English crown and got military support for an invasion of Ireland from the powerful king of France, Louis XIV. William defeated James II at the battle of the Boyne in 1690, and James fled to France while William's armies re-conquered Ireland. This victory is still celebrated by Protestant loyalists today. To prevent any further rebellions, the Irish Catholics were prohibited from holding public office and there were many other restrictions placed on the Catholic Church. Ireland remained a deeply troubled country.

After 1688, many Acts of Parliament permanently changed the balance of power between monarch and Parliament. A new Parliament had to be elected at least every three years (later this became seven years and now it is five years). Every year the monarch had to ask Parliament to renew funding for the army and the navy. In order to govern effectively, the monarch had to have ministers in a Cabinet who could regularly deliver a majority of votes in the two Houses of Parliament. The monarch remained an important political figure for two more centuries but could not insist on policies that Parliament would not support: this is called ' constitutional monarchy'.

## The Act or Treaty of Union

After William III, the monarch's ministers gradually became more important than the monarch. The government of the time was not democratic because men could only vote if they owned property of a certain value, and no women were allowed to vote. Some constituencies had only a few electors and were completely controlled by a single aristocrat who could force the voters to elect whoever he wished. These were called 'pocket boroughs', while small boroughs where the voters could be bribed were called 'rotten boroughs'.

William and Mary's successor, Queen Anne, had no surviving children. The English government became worried that the Scots would choose a different heir to the throne than the English. The English put pressure on the Scots to join England in an Act of Union, called the Treaty of Union in Scotland. This took place in 1707. The kingdoms of England and Scotland became the Kingdom of Great Britain. It had one flag, the Union flag, often called the Union Jack. (The Kingdom of Great Britain became the United Kingdom of Great Britain and Ireland in 1801, after a second Act of Union. In 1922 Ireland split into two - the South became a dominion and the North remained in the Union. The Government of Ireland Act of 1922 created the United Kingdom of Great Britain and Northern Ireland.) While Scotland was no longer an independent country, the Scots obtained trading advantages from union with England while keeping their own legal system and traditional laws, and the Presbyterian Church remained established by law.

## The Prime Minister

When Queen Anne died in 1714, Parliament chose a German, George I, to be the king of Britain, because he was Anne's nearest Protestant relative. The new king still had some political power and influence but was much more dependent on his ministers and their followers who could control Parliament. The members of the House of Commons and the House of Lords called themselves either Whigs or Tories (a name still used today to refer to the modern Conservative Party), but true political parties with mass membership did not emerge until the late 19th century. The most important minister in Parliament became known as the Prime Minister: the first man to hold this office was Sir Robert Walpole, who was Prime Minister for 20 years until 1742.

## The rebellion of the clans

The 18th century was a time of relative peace within Britain. However, in

1745 there was a rebellion in Scotland led by Charles Stuart (Bonnie Prince Charlie), the grandson of James II. He was supported mainly by clansmen in the Highlands in his attempt to regain the British throne for his family. The king's army ruthlessly repressed the power and influence of the clans after defeating them at the battle of Culloden in 1745. The clans lost collective ownership of the land. Chieftains became landlords only through the favour of the English king and clansmen became tenants who had to pay for the land they used. In the 19th century, many landlords destroyed individual small farms or 'crofts' to make space for large flocks of sheep in what were called the 'Highland clearances'. Many people were deported or left for North America as part of the clearances.

## The Enlightenment

Generally, however, the 18th century in Britain was a time of greater domestic peace and tolerance than previously. It was a time of many new ideas in politics, philosophy and science, which together are often called the Enlightenment. Many of the greatest British thinkers of the Enlightenment, such as David Hume and Adam Smith, came from Scotland. Perhaps the most important principles of the Enlightenment were that everyone should have the right to their own political and religious beliefs and that the state should not attempt to dictate in these matters.

## The industrial revolution

Britain was the first country to industrialise on a large scale. Changes in farming, metalworking, mining techniques and the use of steam power brought greater efficiency and increased production. The first large factories were built and many people migrated from the countryside to the cities to work in them. Although many people left Britain and Ireland for the new colonies, the population expanded rapidly. The first Jews to come to Britain since the Middle Ages had settled in London in 1656 and between 1680 and 1720 many refugees came from France. These were called Huguenots. They were Protestants and had been persecuted for their religion. Many were educated and skilled and worked as scientists or in banking, in weaving or other crafts.

At the same time, there was an increase in trade overseas and in colonisation. Britain expanded its power all over the world. Merchants traded with North America and the West Indies, bringing back sugar, tobacco and other goods. Trade in textiles, tea and spices began with India and in the area which today is called Indonesia. The British fought with the Dutch and Spanish traders for a monopoly of trade in the Caribbean. Often, trade led to the annexation of new territories: the East India Company, interested at first only in trading, gradually gained control of vast territories in India in the course of the 18th century.

## The slave trade

There was an evil side to this commercial expansion and prosperity - the Atlantic slave trade. The slave trade had started in the Elizabethan era and was fully established by the 18th century. It was dominated by Britain and the colonies in America. The slave traders bought men and women from West Africa, and British ships took them to work on the sugar and tobacco plantations in America and the Caribbean. The slaves were transported in very bad conditions and many died on the way. Once in the Americas, the slaves became the property of the plantation owners and had to work in appalling conditions. Several cities in the UK, such as Liverpool and Bristol, gained great prosperity as a result of this trade. In 18th-century London, there were numbers of free Africans and escaped slaves, often working as servants or craftsmen. Some wrote books about their experiences.

The conditions of the slaves in the colonies were so bad that many slaves revolted against their owners. Some people in Britain, such as the evangelical Christian William Wilberforce, were opposed to the slave trade. They put pressure on Parliament to abolish slavery. Public opinion gradually turned against the slave trade and in 1807 it became illegal to trade slaves in British ships or from British ports. Later, in 1833, the Emancipation Act abolished slavery throughout the British Empire. After 1833, 2 million Indian and Chinese workers replaced the freed slaves. They worked on sugar plantations in the Caribbean, mines in South Africa, railways in East Africa and in the army in Kenya.

## The American War

In North America the British colonies had prospered and were mainly self-governing. Immigrants from England, Scotland and Ireland had gone to North America looking for a better life and also to escape the dominance of the landlords and of the established church. The notion of liberty was very strong in the colonies. When the British government tried to tax the colonies to pay for their wars in North America against the French and the Native American tribes, the colonies rebelled. They said there should be 'no taxation without representation' in the British Parliament. Parliament refused to compromise. This led the American colonies to declare independence from Britain in 1776. The Declaration of Independence asserted universal principles of free government. Many people in Britain and Europe who wanted political reform welcomed the ideas of the Declaration.

## The second British Empire

The American colonies defeated the British army with the help of the French. After a brief period of peace, wars with France continued, especially after the French Revolution of 1789. Britain's navy at that time was the strongest in Europe. Britain fought against combined French and Spanish fleets, winning the battle of Trafalgar in 1805. In 1815 the French Wars ended with the defeat of the Emperor Napoleon by the Duke of Wellington at Waterloo.

In 1815, Britain ruled territories in Canada, the Caribbean, parts of India, and a few settlements in Australia and southern Africa. A hundred years later, the British Empire had expanded further to cover all of India, Australia and large parts of Africa. Historians call this expansion of the empire after American independence the 'Second British Empire'. It became the largest in the world, with an estimated population of over 400 million people.

As the empire developed, many people left the United Kingdom to find new opportunities overseas. Many settled in South Africa, Canada, Australia, New Zealand and the United States. Between 1853 and 1913, as many as 13 million British citizens left the country. There were also many migrants to Britain from various parts of the world. For example, between 1870 and 1914, around 120,000 Russian and Polish Jews came to Britain to escape persecution at home. Many settled in London's East End and in Manchester and Leeds.

## Industry and political reform

British industry led the world in the 19th century. In the late 18th century there had been a boom in the building of canals. These linked the factories in the cities to the ports. In the early 19th century, George and Robert Stephenson pioneered the railway engine and the building of the railways began. There were also great advances in other areas such as the building of bridges by engineers like Isambard Kingdom Brunel. Much of the heavy work of creating Britain's industrial infrastructure was done by immigrant labour from Ireland. Many Irish people migrated to England to escape famine and poverty and settled as agricultural workers and labourers. By 1861 there were large populations of Irish people in cities such as Liverpool, London, Manchester and Glasgow.

## The right to vote

The aristocracy still dominated Parliament but there was a challenge from the growing commercial and entrepreneurial middle class in the newly wealthy industrial towns and cities. The power of this new middle class led to the Reform Act of 1832. The right to vote was still based

on property but the number of people entitled to vote was greatly increased. The Act also abolished many ancient constituencies with few voters and gave more parliamentary seats to the cities. This began a permanent shift of power away from the landed interests of the aristocracy to the interests of the cities.

After 1832, the working classes and other people without property began to demand the right to vote. The leaders of this movement were called the Chartists. Although the Chartists failed, a generation later the intense rivalry between the Conservative Party (led by Benjamin Disraeli) and the Liberal Party (led by

William Gladstone) resulted in the creation of many more urban seats in Parliament and a further lowering of the property qualifications to vote. Although the 1867 Reform Act again expanded the number of voters, still only a third of men (and no women) were allowed to vote. These numbers were enough, however, to force the leaders of the political parties to create organisations to reach out to ordinary voters. This was the beginning of something like democratic politics. Even so, universal suffrage (the right of everyone to vote) took much longer. It was not until 1928 that all men and women had the right to vote. The right of women to vote

was won after a long campaign by the Women's Suffrage Movement (the Suffragettes) who had to resort to civil disobedience to achieve their goals.

## Imperial uncertainties

In the late 19th century, the Conservative Party favoured the expansion of the British Empire. Disraeli promoted the empire by making Queen Victoria Empress of India in 1876. The Liberals were more uncertain about the empire and were influenced by stories of poverty and the mistreatment of the populations of the colonies. Liberals believed that the empire had become over-large and would soon collapse because of this. They thought the

### The First World War

continuous wars in many parts of the empire such as India's northwest frontier or southern Africa, were futile. The Conservatives, by contrast, believed that trade and commerce needed military security and law and order. They also believed that the colonies benefited from the influence of the British.

The Boer War of 1899 to 1902 made both viewpoints more entrenched. The British expanded into South Africa to control the gold mines of the Transvaal, which had been colonised by settlers from the Netherlands called the Boers. The Boers resisted and it took massive manpower resources from the empire to defeat them. To some imperialists this

showed the unity of the empire but to others it was a warning that the empire would eventually collapse. The British Empire did finally come to an end as a result of events in the 20th century.

At the beginning of the century there was a mood of optimism in Britain. Local government was reformed on a more democratic basis. Retirement pensions for the poor and financial help for the unemployed were provided by the government, and a new political party, the Labour Party, arose to represent the interests of the working classes in Parliament and local government. There was a general belief in modernity and progress. That belief was shattered when a terrible war broke out between several European nations. This was the First World War (1914 -18). Millions of people were killed or wounded. One battle alone, the British attack on the

Somme in 1916, resulted in about 400,000 British casualties and probably the same number of Germans. The whole of the British Empire was involved in the fighting: for example, over 1 million Indians fought on behalf of the UK all over the world. Around 40,000 were killed. Men from the West Indies, Africa, Australia, New Zealand and Canada also fought on behalf of the British.

### The partition of Ireland

Ireland had been unified with Great Britain by the Act of Union in 1801. The 19th century had been a very difficult period in Irish history. In the middle of the 19th century, the potato crop had failed, and Ireland suffered a famine. This caused huge numbers of deaths from disease and starvation and many people had to leave Ireland. The government in London failed to help the Irish people adequately, causing bitterness that still continues. The Irish nationalist movement grew stronger during this period. Some, such as the Fenians, favoured complete independence. Others, such as Charles Stuart Parnell, advocated 'Home Rule' (devolution). In 1913, the British government finally promised Home Rule for Ireland and the Home Rule Bill started to go through Parliament, but the Protestants in the North of Ireland, who were descendants of the settlers introduced in the 17th-

century plantations, threatened to resist Home Rule by force of arms. Because of the outbreak of the First World War, the British government postponed the changes it had promised to Ireland. In 1916, however, there was an uprising (the Easter Rising) against the British by Irish nationalists in Dublin. The leaders of the uprising were executed under military law. This only strengthened the support for nationalism in Ireland and led to a guerrilla war against the British army and the police. In 1921 a peace treaty was signed and in 1922 Ireland was separated into two parts. The six counties in the North, which were mainly Protestant,

remained part of the United Kingdom, while the rest of Ireland became the Irish Free State and became a republic in 1949. Some people in both parts of Ireland were opposed to this compromise and still wished for independence for the whole of Ireland. This has caused many years of conflict in the North. This conflict, between those wishing for full Irish independence and those wishing to remain loyal to the British government, is sometimes called the 'Troubles'. Only recently has peace returned to Northern Ireland.

## The inter-war period

In the 1920s there were improvements in public

housing and a general rise in living standards, but the worldwide 'Great Depression' from 1929 created mass unemployment, and the 1930s were a time of economic depression and crisis. British Prime Ministers in the 1930s failed to understand the seriousness of the threat of the German dictator and leader of the Nazi party, Adolf Hitler. The British tried to make concessions to Hitler, in a policy known as 'appeasement'. Many people in the UK blamed the Conservative Prime Ministers of the time for being too complacent towards Hitler and his expansionist ambitions and racist ideology. The British government realised it had

## The Second World War

to go to war against Germany when Hitler invaded Poland in 1939. In the first year of war, Hitler's armies successfully invaded Belgium, France and the Netherlands. In this national crisis, Winston Churchill became Prime Minister and Britain's war leader.

The Germans prepared to invade the United Kingdom but before they could do this they needed to control the air. The British resisted the German air force with their fighter planes, Spitfires and Hurricanes, and won the crucial aerial battle against the Germans called the 'Battle of Britain'. Even so, the German air force was able to continue night-time bombing of London and of other British cities such as Coventry, which was nearly totally destroyed. Churchill encouraged a national spirit of resistance in the United Kingdom. In the Far East, however, the British were defeated in Singapore by the Japanese, who were allies of Germany. The Japanese then occupied

Burma and threatened India.

When the Japanese bombed the United States naval base at Pearl Harbor, the USA entered the war. The allied forces gradually gained the upper hand, winning victories in North Africa and Italy, while the Germans lost millions of soldiers as a result of their attack on Russia in 1942. Finally, the Allies were strong enough to attack the Germans in Western Europe in the D-Day landings of 1944. After bitter fighting on the beaches of Normandy, they pressed on through France and into Germany. With their Russian allies they brought about the total defeat of Germany

in the summer of 1945. The war against Japan was ended when the United States exploded its newly developed atom bombs over the cities of Hiroshima and Nagasaki a few weeks later. Although it had played an important role in winning the war, the UK was exhausted economically. Liberation or self-government movements grew stronger and more successful in India and other colonies.

# Politics in Britain since 1945

## The welfare state

In 1945 the British people elected a Labour government, despite Churchill's success as war leader. The new Prime Minister was Clement Attlee. The government established a free National Health Service (NHS) which guaranteed a minimum standard of healthcare for all. Unemployment reduced rapidly. The railways, coal mines, gas, water and electricity supplies were put under public ownership (nationalised).

The Labour Party also believed in self-government for the former colonies and so granted independence to India, Pakistan, and Ceylon (now Sri Lanka) in 1947. Other colonies in Africa, the Caribbean and the Pacific achieved independence over the next 20 years.

The Labour government provided for the UK's defence by developing its own atomic bomb and joining the new North Atlantic Treaty Organisation (NATO), an alliance of nations set up to resist the perceived threat of invasion by the Soviet Union and its allies.

## Domestic policies 1951-79

In 1951 Labour was defeated. The government had demanded too much austerity and restraint as the UK recovered after the war. After 1951, Conservative governments made few changes to the new nationalised institutions and to the welfare state which had been introduced by Labour. The country was run under a 'mixed economy', a free market within a framework of public ownership of key utilities, transport and communications. A failed invasion of Suez in 1956 showed that Britain could no longer rely on military power to protect its global economic interests. Even so, the 1950s were a period of increasing prosperity. The Prime Minister of the day summed this up in a phrase that is still quoted: 'You've never had it so good.'

The Labour Party returned to power from 1964 to 1970 and then again from 1974 to 1979, but the UK now faced many economic problems such as inflation, unstable international currency exchange rates and the 'balance of payments' (importing more than it paid for in exports). There was also a shortage of labour and, from the 1940s onwards, governments encouraged the arrival in the UK of immigrant workers from the former colonies in the Indian subcontinent and the Caribbean.

This was a time of conflict between the government and the trade unions. Many believed that the unions had too much power and that they restrained government and business. Both Conservative and

Labour governments faced many large-scale strikes during the 1970s which did much to destroy confidence in the British economy. It was at this time, too, that the tensions between the communities in Northern Ireland flared into violence which led to the controversial deployment of the army there and the suspension, in 1972, of the original Northern Ireland Parliament. Some 3,000 lives of civilians and security personnel were lost in the decades after 1969.

## The Common Market

Meanwhile, West Germany, France, Belgium, Italy, Luxembourg and the Netherlands had formed the European Economic Community (EEC). The EEC had the goal of harmonising political, economic and trade relations between its members and creating a common agricultural policy. It also planned to make the borders free between its member states. A European Parliament was established in Strasbourg and a civil service, called the European Commission, in Brussels. At first the UK did not wish to join the EEC. Many British politicians believed that the links between the UK and the USA and the empire were more important and that the Commonwealth could form an economic bloc based on sterling, but this policy wrongly assumed that the countries of the Commonwealth wished to be tied to the UK economically. When the British government did decide that it wanted to join, its applications were vetoed twice, first in 1963 and again in 1967. The French President, Charles de Gaulle, was not convinced that the UK was committed to the aims of the EEC as these had developed without British involvement. De Gaulle also believed that the UK's influence would be too great, and that its closeness to the United States, both culturally and economically, would undermine those aims.

In 1972, the Conservative Prime Minister Edward Heath negotiated the UK's entry into the EEC. The country was still divided on the issue of joining, and this led the next Labour government to hold a referendum in 1975, in which the majority voted to continue its membership. Since then, many more European countries have joined, including many countries in Eastern Europe. In 1992, the Treaty of Maastricht renamed the EEC and its related institutions, the European Union (EU) (see chapter 4).

## The Thatcher era

The Conservatives won the general election in 1979 and remained in office until 1997. Under Margaret

## New Labour

Thatcher, Prime Minister from 1979 until 1990, the government returned to the principles of a strict control of the money supply and a free market economy. The Conservatives privatised the main nationalised industries and public services: electricity, gas, water, telephones and the railways. The power of the trade unions was greatly reduced by new legislation restricting the right to strike. The Conservatives gave people who lived in municipal housing (council houses) the right to buy their homes. This led to a much lower stock of public housing by the 1990s. Mrs Thatcher's economic policies controlled inflation but some believed they

also caused a massive decline in industry. Others, however, say this was caused by foreign competition. At this time there was also a great increase in the role of the City of London as an international centre for investments, insurance and other financial services. The invasion by Argentina of the Falkland Islands in 1982 was unforeseen, but military action led to the recovery of the islands. The war and her way of defending her sense of the UK's interests in the European Union established Mrs Thatcher's credentials as a national leader with many voters, although for many others she remained a divisive figure.

In 1997 the Conservatives were beaten in the general election by the Labour Party, now branded New Labour to emphasise the changes it had undergone since its years of power in the 1970s. New Labour, led by Tony Blair, wished to break from the old Labour policies of public ownership and high taxation for public services. It did not re-nationalise any of the services or industries which had been privatised by the Conservatives. Its goals were to make existing public services such as education and health more efficient and more accountable. Labour, like the Conservatives, favoured partnerships between the public and private sectors. The arguments were no

longer whether public utilities should be privately or publicly owned, but about the right mix of public and private enterprise.

The Blair government broke with Conservative policy by introducing a Scottish Parliament and a Welsh Assembly (see chapter 4). The Scottish Parliament has substantial powers to legislate. The Welsh Assembly has fewer legislative powers but considerable control over public services. In Northern Ireland the Blair government was able to build on the Conservatives' success in negotiating an end to the 'Troubles' which had afflicted the province since 1969 and, in co-operation with the Irish government, to seek political agreement among the nationalist, unionist, and other parties. This, however, has proved more elusive, and arrangements for devolution, agreed in 1998, have been interrupted and are currently suspended.

## Today

Today's government faces several issues. Some of the problems are international, such as global warming, terrorism, and the violence in Iraq. Other debates are domestic such as disagreements over taxation, pensions, law and order, health, education, immigration and asylum.

The United Kingdom is perhaps more socially mobile and less class conscious than it was in the past. People have better health than in previous generations and tend to live longer. Although there is still great inequality between the very rich and poor, people are generally wealthier in real terms. The UK is also a more pluralistic society than it was 100 years ago, both in ethnic and religious terms. Post-war immigration means that nearly 10% of the population has a parent or grandparent born outside the UK. Racism remains a problem in some areas, although it is actively combated both in opinion and in law and most

people believe that it has diminished. The UK has been a multi-national and multi-cultural society for a long time, without this being a threat to its British identity, or its English, Scottish, Welsh or Irish cultural and national identities.

# Chapter 2

# A CHANGING SOCIETY

## Migration to Britain

In this chapter there is information about:

### Migration to Britain

- The long history of immigration to the United Kingdom

- Different reasons why people migrated to the UK

- Basic changes in immigration patterns over the last 30 years

### The changing role of women

- Changes to family structures and women's rights since the 19th century

- Women's campaigns for rights, including the right to vote, in the late 19th and early 20th centuries

- Discrimination against women in the workplace and in education

- Changing attitudes to women working, and responsibilities of men and women in the home

### Children, family and young people

- The identity, interests, tastes and lifestyle patterns of children and young people

- Education and work

- Health hazards: cigarettes, alcohol and illegal drugs

- Young people's political and social attitudes

Many people living in Britain today have their origins in other countries. They can trace their roots to regions throughout the world such as Europe, the Middle East, Africa, Asia and the Caribbean. In the distant past, invaders came to Britain, seized land and stayed (see chapter 1). More recently, people come to Britain to find safety, jobs and a better life.

Britain is proud of its tradition of offering safety to people who are escaping persecution and hardship. For example, in the 16th and 18th centuries, Huguenots (French Protestants) came to Britain to escape religious persecution in France. In the mid -1840s there was a terrible famine in Ireland and many Irish people migrated to Britain. Many Irish men became labourers and helped to build canals and railways across Britain.

From 1880 to 1910, a large number of Jewish people came to Britain to escape racist attacks (called 'pogroms') in what was then called the Russian Empire and from the countries now called Poland, Ukraine and Belarus.

### Migration since 1945

After the Second World War (1939-45), there was a huge task of rebuilding Britain. There were not enough people to do the work, so the British government encouraged workers from Ireland and other parts of Europe to come to the UK to help with the reconstruction. In 1948, people from the West Indies were also invited to come and work.

During the 1950s, there was still a shortage of labour in the UK. The UK encouraged immigration in the 1950s for economic reasons and many industries advertised for workers from overseas. For example, centres were set up in the West Indies to recruit people to drive buses. Textile and engineering firms from the north of England and the Midlands sent agents to India and Pakistan to find workers. For about 25 years, people from the West Indies, India, Pakistan, and later Bangladesh, travelled to work and settle in Britain.

The number of people migrating from these areas fell in the late 1960s and early 70s because the government passed new laws to restrict immigration to Britain, although immigrants from 'old' Commonwealth countries such as Australia, New Zealand and Canada did not have to face such strict controls.

## Check that you understand:

- Some of the historical reasons for immigration to the UK

- Some of the reasons for immigration to the UK since 1945

- The main immigrant groups coming to the UK since 1945, the countries they came from and kind of work they did

During this time, however, the UK was able to help a large number of refugees. In 1972 the UK accepted thousands of people of Indian origin who had been forced to leave Uganda. Another programme to help people from Vietnam was introduced in the late 1970s. Since 1979, more than 25,000 refugees from South East Asia have been allowed to settle in the UK.

In the 1980s the largest immigrant groups were from the United States, Australia, South Africa, and New Zealand. In the early 1990s, groups of people from the former Soviet Union came to Britain looking for a new and safer way of life. Since 1994 there has been a global rise in mass migration for both political and economic reasons.

## The changing role of women

In 19th-century Britain, families were usually large and in many poorer homes men, women and children all contributed towards the family income. Although they made an important economic contribution, women in Britain had fewer rights than men. Until 1857, a married woman had no right to divorce her husband. Until 1882, when a woman got married, her earnings, property and money automatically belonged to her husband.

In the late 19th and early 20th centuries, an increasing number of women campaigned and demonstrated for greater rights and, in particular, the right to vote. They became known as 'Suffragettes'. These protests decreased during the First World War because women joined in the war effort and therefore did a much greater variety of work than they had before. When the First World War ended in 1918, women over the age of 30 were finally given the right to vote and to stand for election to Parliament. It was not until 1928 that women won the right to vote at 21, at the same age as men.

Despite these improvements, women still faced discrimination in the workplace. For example, it was quite common for employers to ask women to leave their jobs when they got married. Many jobs were closed to women and it was difficult for women to enter universities. During the 1960s and 1970s there was increasing pressure from women for equal rights. Parliament passed new laws giving women the right to equal pay and prohibiting employers from discriminating against women because of their sex (see also chapter 6).

## Women in Britain today

Women in Britain today make up 51% of the population and 45% of the workforce. These days girls leave school, on average, with better qualifications than boys and there are now more women than men at university.

Employment opportunities for women are now much greater than they were in the past. Although women continue to be employed in traditional female areas such as healthcare, teaching, secretarial and retail work, there is strong evidence that attitudes are changing, and women are now active in a much wider range of work than before. Research shows that very few people today believe that women in Britain should stay at home and not go out to work. Today, almost three-quarters of women with school-age children are in paid work.

In most households, women continue to have the main responsibility for childcare and housework. There is evidence that there is now greater equality in homes and that more men are taking some responsibility for raising the family and doing housework. Despite this progress, many people believe that more needs to be done to achieve greater equality for women. There are still examples of discrimination against women, particularly in the workplace, despite the laws that exist to prevent it. Women still do not always have the same access to promotion and better-paid jobs. The average hourly pay rate for women is 20% less than for men, and after leaving university most women still earn less than men.

### Check that you understand:

- When women aged over 30 were first given the right to vote

- When women were given equal voting rights with men

- Some of the important developments to create equal rights in the workplace

# Children, family and young people

In the UK, there are almost 15 million children and young people up to the age of 19. This is almost one-quarter of the UK population.

Over the last 20 years, family patterns in Britain have been transformed because of changing attitudes towards divorce and separation. Today, 65% of children live with both birth parents, almost 25% live in lone-parent families, and 10% live within a stepfamily. Most children in Britain receive weekly pocket money from their parents and many get extra money for doing jobs around the house.

Children in the UK do not play outside the home as much as they did in the past. Part of the reason for this is increased home entertainment such as television, videos and computers. There is also increased concern for children's safety and there are many stories in newspapers about child molestation by strangers, but there is no evidence that this kind of danger is increasing.

Young people have different identities, interests and fashions to older people. Many young people move away from their family home when they become adults but this varies from one community to another.

## Education

The law states that children between the ages of 5 and 16 must attend school. The tests that pupils take are very important, and in England and Scotland children take national tests in English, mathematics and science when they are 7, 11 and 14 years old. (In Wales, teachers assess children's progress when they are 7 and 11 and they take a national test at the age of 14). The tests give important information about children's progress and achievement, the subjects they are doing well in and the areas where they need extra help.

Most young people take the General Certificate of Secondary Education (GCSE), or, in Scotland, Scottish Qualifications Authority (SQA) Standard Grade examinations when they are 16. At 17 and 18, many take vocational qualifications, General Certificates of Education at an Advanced level (AGCEs), AS level units or Higher/Advanced Higher Grades in Scotland. Schools and colleges will expect good GCSE or SQA Standard Grade results before allowing a student to enrol on an AGCE or Scottish Higher/Advanced Higher course.

AS levels are Advanced Subsidiary qualifications gained by completing three AS units. Three AS units are considered as one-half of an AGCE. In the second part of the course, three more AS units can be studied to complete the AGCE qualification.

Many people refer to AGCEs by the old name of A levels. AGCEs are the traditional route for entry to higher education courses, but many higher education students enter with different kinds of qualifications.

One in three young people now go on to higher education at college or university. Some young people defer their university entrance for a year and take a 'gap year'. This year out of education often includes voluntary work and travel overseas. Some young people work to earn and save money to pay for their university fees and living expenses.

People over 16 years of age may also choose to study at Colleges of Further Education or Adult Education Centres. There is a wide range of academic and vocational courses available as well as courses which develop leisure interests and skills. Contact your local college for details.

## Work

It is common for young people to have a part-time job while they are still at school. It is thought there are 2 million children at work at any one time. The most common jobs are newspaper delivery and work in supermarkets and newsagents. Many parents believe that part-time work helps children to become more independent as well as providing them (and sometimes their families) with extra income. There are laws about the age when children can take up paid work (usually not before 14), the type of work they can do and the number of hours they can work (see www.worksmart.org.uk for more information).

It is very important to note that there are concerns for the safety of children who work illegally or who are not properly supervised and the employment of children is strictly controlled by law (see also pages 84 and 85).

## Health hazards

Many parents worry that their children may misuse drugs and addictive substances.

## Smoking:

Although cigarette smoking is slowly falling in the adult population, more young people are smoking, and more school age girls smoke than boys. From 1 October 2007 it is illegal to sell tobacco products to anyone under 18 years old. Smoking is generally not allowed in public buildings and work places throughout the UK.

## Alcohol:

Young people under the age of 18 are not allowed to buy alcohol in Britain, but there is concern about the age some young people start drinking alcohol and the amount of alcohol they drink at one time, known as 'binge drinking'. It is illegal to be drunk in public and there are now more penalties to help control this problem, including on-the-spot fines.

## Illegal drugs:

As in most countries, it is illegal to possess drugs such as heroin, cocaine, ecstasy, amphetamines and cannabis. Current statistics show that half of all young adults, and about a third of the population as a whole, have used illegal drugs at one time or another.

There is a strong link between the use of hard drugs (e.g. crack cocaine and heroin) and crime, and also hard drugs and mental illness. The misuse of drugs has a huge social and financial cost for the country. This is a serious issue and British society needs to find an effective way of dealing with the problem.

**Check that you understand:**

- The proportion of all young people who go on to higher education

- Lifestyle patterns of children and young people (e.g. pocket money, leaving home on reaching adulthood)

- Changing family patterns and attitudes to changing family patterns (e.g. divorce)

- That education in Britain is free and compulsory, and that there is compulsory testing (in England and Scotland) at ages 7, 11 and 14; there are also GSCE and/ or vocational exams at 16; and Advanced level exams (A and AS) at ages 17 and 18

- That there is a government target that half of all young people attend higher education

- That there are strict laws regarding the employment of children

- That there are important health concerns and laws relating to children and young people and smoking, alcohol and drugs

- That young people are eligible to vote in elections from age 18

## Young people's political and social attitudes

Young people in Britain can vote in elections from the age
of 18. In the 2001 general election, however, only 1 in 5
first-time voters used their vote. There has been a great
debate over the reasons for this. Some researchers think
that one reason is that young people are not interested in
the political process.

Although most young people show little interest in party
politics, there is strong evidence that many are interested
in specific political issues such as the environment and
cruelty to animals.

In 2003 a survey of young people in England and Wales
showed that they believe the five most important issues
in Britain were crime, drugs, war/terrorism, racism and
health. The same survey asked young people about their
participation in political and community events. They
found that 86 % of young people had taken part in some
form of community event over the past year, and 50% had
taken part in fund-raising or collecting money for charity.
Similar results have been found in surveys in Scotland and
Northern Ireland. Many children first get involved in these
activities while at school where they study Citizenship as
part of the National Curriculum.

Check that you understand the key terms and vocabulary for this chapter

## Migration to Britain:

- migrate, immigrate, immigration, immigrant
- persecution, famine, conflict
- labour, labourer
- recruit
- restrict
- political asylum
- the war effort

## Changing role of women:

- income, earnings
- rights, equal rights
- campaign, demonstrate
- discriminate, discrimination
- prohibit
- workforce
- household
- promotion

## Children, family and young people:

- eligible
- concern
- molestation
- attitudes
- hazards
- birth parent, stepfamily
- compulsory
- informal
- methods of assessment
- defer
- gap year
- independent
- income
- misuse
- addictive substances
- abuse
- binge drinking
- on-the-spot fines
- controlled drugs
- criminal offence
- possess

- heroin, cocaine, crack cocaine, ecstasy, amphetamines, cannabis
- burglary, mugging
- debate
- politicians, political process, party politics, political issues
- specific
- concern
- environment
- terrorism, racism
- participation
- fund-raising

# Chapter 3

# UK TODAY: A PROFILE

## Population

In this chapter there is information about:

- The population of the UK

- The census

- Ethnic diversity

- The regions of Britain

- Religion and religious freedom

- Customs and traditions

In 2005 the population of the United Kingdom was just under 60 million people.

**UK population 2005**

| | | |
|---|---|---|
| England | (84% of the population) | 50.1 million |
| Scotland | (8% of the population) | 5.1 million |
| Wales | (5% of the population) | 2.9 million |
| N. Ireland | (3% of the population) | 1.7 million |
| Total UK | | 59.8 million |

Source: National Statistics

The population has grown by 7.7% since 1971, and growth has been faster in more recent years. Although the general population in the UK has increased in the last 20 years, in some areas such as the North East and North West of England there has been a decline.

Both the birth rate and the death rate are falling and as a result the UK now has an ageing population. For instance, there are more people over 60 than children under 16. There is also a record number of people aged 85 and over.

## The census

A census is a count of the whole population. It also collects statistics on topics such as age, place of birth, occupation, ethnicity, housing, health, and marital status.

A census has been taken every ten years since 1801, except during the Second World War. The next census will take place in 2011.

During a census, a form is delivered to every household in the country. This form asks for detailed information about each member of the household and must be completed by law. The information remains confidential and anonymous; it can only be released to the public after 100 years, when many people researching their family history find it very useful. General census information is used to identify population trends and to help planning. More information about the census, the census form and statistics from previous censuses can be found at www.statistics.gov.uk/census

## Ethnic diversity

The UK population is ethnically diverse and is changing rapidly, especially in large cities such as London, so it is not always easy to get an exact picture of the ethnic origin of all the population from census statistics. Each of the four countries of the UK (England, Wales, Scotland and Northern Ireland) has different customs, attitudes and histories.

People of Indian, Pakistani, Chinese, Black Caribbean, Black African, Bangladeshi and mixed ethnic descent make up 8.3% of the UK population. Today about half the members of these communities were born in the United Kingdom.

There are also considerable numbers of people resident in the UK who are of Irish, Italian, Greek and Turkish Cypriot, Polish, Australian, Canadian, New Zealand and American descent. Large numbers have also arrived since 2004 from the new East European member states of the European Union. These groups are not identified separately in the census statistics in the following table.

## UK population 2001

| | Million | UK population % |
|---|---|---|
| **White** (a people of European, Australian, American descent) | 54.2 | 92 |
| **Mixed** | 0.7 | 1.2 |
| **Asian or Asian British** | | |
| Indian | 1.1 | 1.8 |
| Pakistani | 0.7 | 1.3 |
| Bangladeshi | 0.3 | 0.5 |
| Other Asian | 0.2 | 0.4 |
| **Black or Black British** | | |
| Black Caribbean | 0.6 | 1.0 |
| Black African | 0.5 | 0.8 |
| Black other | 0.1 | 0.2 |
| **Chinese** | 0.2 | 0.4 |
| **Other** | 0.2 | 0.4 |

Source: National Statistics from the 2001 census

## Where do the largest ethnic minority groups live?

The figures from the 2001 census show that most members of the large ethnic minority groups in the UK live in England, where they make up 9% of the total population. 45% of all ethnic minority people live in the London area, where they form nearly one-third of the population (29%). Other areas of England with large ethnic minority populations are the West Midlands, the South East, the North West, and Yorkshire and Humberside.

Proportion of ethnic minority groups in the countries of the UK

| | | | |
|---|---|---|---|
| England | 9% | Wales | 2% |
| Scotland | 2% | Northern Ireland | less than 1% |

# The nations and regions of the UK

The UK is a medium-sized country. The longest distance on the mainland, from John O'Groats on the north coast of Scotland to Land's End in the south-west corner of England, is about 870 miles (approximately 1,400 kilometres). Most of the population live in towns and cities.

There are many variations in culture and language in the different parts of the United Kingdom. This is seen in differences in architecture, in some local customs, in types of food, and especially in language. The English language has many accents and dialects. These are a clear indication of regional differences in the UK. Well-known dialects in England are Geordie (Tyneside), Scouse (Liverpool) and Cockney (London). Many other languages in addition to English are spoken in the UK, especially in multicultural cities.

In Wales, Scotland and Northern Ireland, people speak different varieties and dialects of English. In Wales, too, an increasing number of people speak Welsh, which is taught in schools and universities. In Scotland Gaelic is spoken in some parts of the Highlands and Islands and in Northern Ireland a few people speak Irish Gaelic. Some of the dialects of English spoken in Scotland show the influence of the old Scottish language, Scots. One of the dialects spoken in Northern Ireland is called Ulster Scots.

**Check that you understand:**

- The size of the current UK population

- The population of Scotland, Wales and Northern Ireland

- What the census is and when the next one will be

- What the largest ethnic minorities in the UK are

- Where most ethnic minority people live

- What languages other than English are spoken in Wales, Scotland and Northern Ireland

- Some of the ways you can identify regional differences in the UK

# Religion

Although the UK is historically a Christian society, everyone has the legal right to practise the religion of their choice. In the 2001 census, just over 75% said they had a religion: 7 out of 10 of these were Christians. There were also a considerable number of people who followed other religions. Although many people in the UK said they held religious beliefs, currently only around 10% of the population attend religious services. More people attend services in Scotland and Northern Ireland than in England and Wales. In London the number of people who attend religious services is increasing.

| Religions in the UK | % |
|---|---|
| Christian (10% of whom are Roman Catholic) | 71.6 |
| Muslim | 2.7 |
| Hindu | 1.0 |
| Sikh | 0.6 |
| Jewish | 0.5 |
| Buddhist | 0.3 |
| Other | 0.3 |
| Total All | 77 |
| No religion | 15.5 |
| Not stated | 7.3 |

Source: National Statistics from the 2001 census

## The Christian Churches

In England there is a constitutional link between church and state. The official church of the state is the Church of England. The Church of England is called the Anglican Church in other countries and the Episcopal Church in Scotland and in the USA. The Church of England is a Protestant church and has existed since the Reformation in the 1530s (see chapter 1 for explanation). The king or queen (the monarch) is the head, or Supreme Governor, of the Church of England. The monarch is not allowed to marry anyone who is not Protestant. The spiritual leader of the Church of England is the Archbishop of Canterbury. The monarch has the right to select the Archbishop and other senior church officials, but usually the choice is made by the Prime Minister and a committee appointed by the Church. Several Church of England bishops sit in the House of Lords (see chapter 4). The Church of Scotland is Presbyterian, national and free from state control. It has no bishops and is governed for spiritual purposes by a series of courts, so its most senior representative is the Moderator (chairperson) of its annual General Assembly. There is no established church in Wales or in Northern Ireland.

Other Protestant Christian groups in the UK are Baptists, Presbyterians, Methodists and Quakers. 10% of Christians are Roman Catholic (40% in Northern Ireland).

## Patron saints

England, Scotland, Wales and Northern Ireland each have a national saint called a patron saint. Each saint has a feast day. In the past these were celebrated as holy days when many people had a day off work. Today these are not public holidays except for 17 March in Northern Ireland.

### Patron saints' days

| | |
|---|---|
| St. David's day, Wales | 1 March |
| St. Patrick's day, Northern Ireland | 17 March |
| St. George's day, England | 23 April |
| St. Andrew's day, Scotland | 30 November |

There are four 'Bank Holidays' and four other public holidays a year (most people call all these holidays Bank Holidays). There are other public holidays in Scotland and Northern Ireland.

## Customs and traditions

### Festivals

Throughout the year there are festivals of art, music and culture, such as the Notting Hill Carnival in west London and the Edinburgh Festival. Customs and traditions from various religions, such as Eid ul-Fitr (Muslim), Diwali (Hindu) and Hanukkah (Jewish) are widely recognised in the UK. Children learn about these at school. The main Christian festivals are Christmas and Easter. There are also celebrations of non-religious traditions such as New Year.

**Check that you understand:**

- The percentage (%) of the UK population who say they are Christian

- How many people say they have no religion

- What percentage are Muslim, Hindu, Sikh, Jewish, Buddhist

- Everyone in the UK has the right to practise their religion

- The Anglican Church, or Church of England, is the church of the state in England (established church)

- The monarch (king or queen) is head of the Church of England

- In Scotland the established church is the Presbyterian Church of Scotland. In Wales and Northern Ireland there is no established church

## The main Christian festivals

### Christmas Day

25 December, celebrates the birth of Jesus Christ. It is a public holiday. Many Christians go to church on Christmas Eve (24 December) or on Christmas Day itself. Christmas is also usually celebrated by people who are not Christian. People usually spend the day at home and eat a special meal, which often includes turkey. They give each other gifts, send each other cards and decorate their houses. Many people decorate a tree. Christmas is a special time for children. Very young children believe that an old man, Father Christmas (or Santa Claus), brings them presents during the night. He is always shown in pictures with a long white beard, dressed in red. Boxing Day, 26 December, is the day after Christmas. It is a public holiday. Easter is also an important Christian festival.

## Other festivals and traditions

### New Year

1 January, is a public holiday. People usually celebrate on the night of 31 December. In Scotland, 31 December is called Hogmanay and 2 January is also a public holiday. In Scotland Hogmanay is a bigger holiday for some people than Christmas.

### Valentine's Day

14 February, is when lovers exchange cards and gifts. Sometimes people send anonymous cards to someone they secretly admire.

### April Fool's Day

1 April, is a day when people play jokes on each other until midday. Often TV and newspapers carry stories intended to deceive credulous viewers and readers.

### Mother's Day

The Sunday three weeks before Easter is a day when children send cards or buy gifts for their mothers.

### Hallowe'en

31 October, is a very ancient festival. Young people will often dress up in frightening costumes to play 'trick or treat'. Giving them sweets or chocolates might stop them playing a trick on you. Sometimes people carry lanterns made out of pumpkins with a candle inside.

### Guy Fawkes Night

5 November, is an occasion when people in Great Britain set off fireworks at home or in special displays. The origin of this celebration was an event in 1605, when a group of Catholics led by Guy Fawkes failed in their plan to kill the Protestant king with a bomb in the Houses of Parliament.

### Remembrance Day

11 November, commemorates those who died fighting in the First and Second World Wars, and other wars. Many people wear poppies (a red flower) in memory of those who died. At 11 a.m. there is a two-minute silence.

## Sport

Sport of all kinds plays a important part in many people's lives. Football, tennis, rugby and cricket are very popular sports in the UK. There are no United Kingdom teams for football and rugby. England, Scotland, Wales and Northern Ireland have their own teams. Important sporting events include the Grand National horse race, the Football Association (FA) cup final (and equivalents in Northern Ireland, Scotland and Wales), the Open golf championship and the Wimbledon tennis tournament.

**Check that you understand:**

- Which sports are most popular in the UK

- The patron saints' days in England, Scotland, Wales and Northern Ireland

- What Bank Holidays are

- The main traditional festivals in the UK

- That the main festivals in the UK are Christian based, but that important festivals from other religions are recognised and explained to children in schools

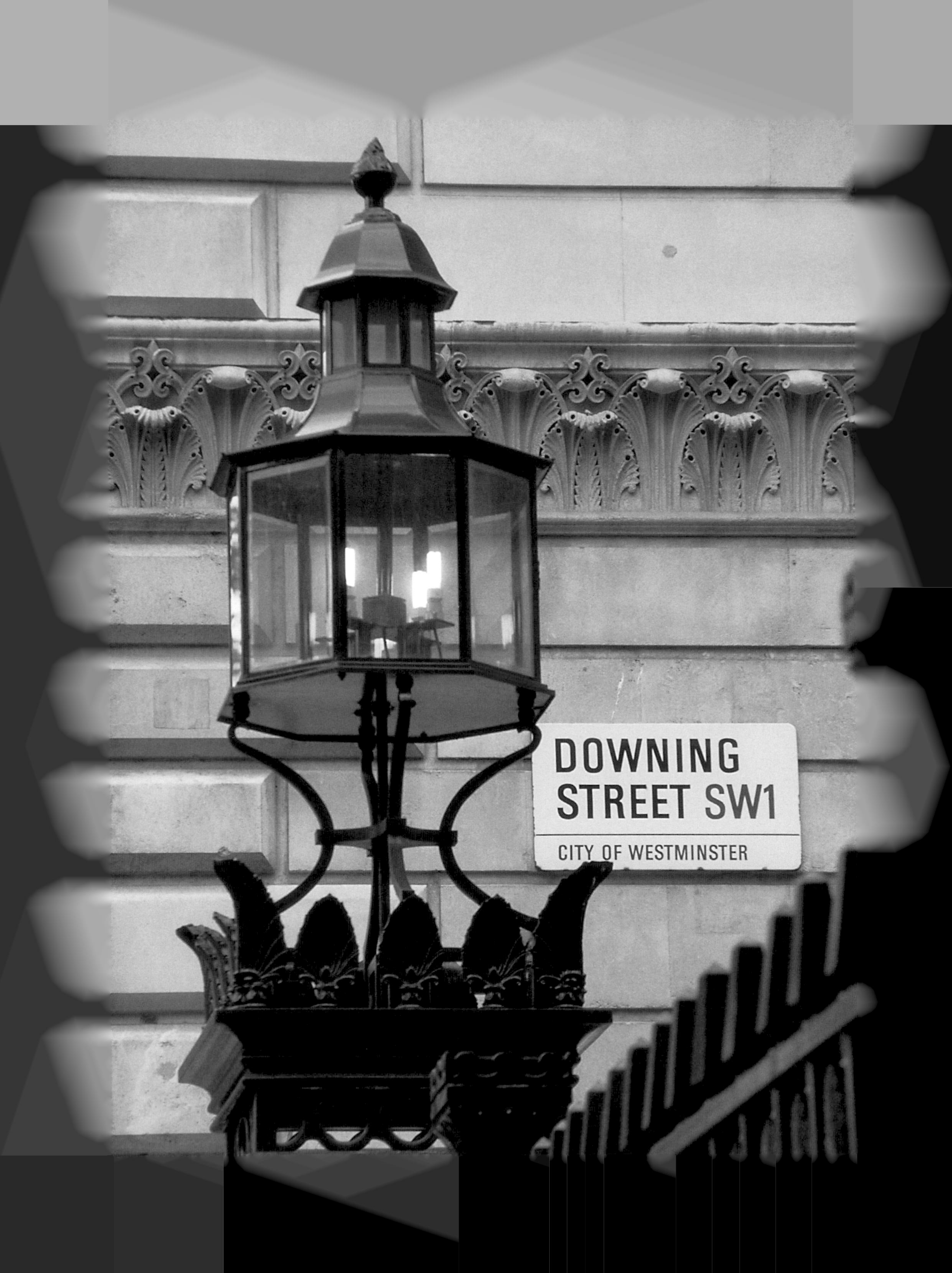
DOWNING
STREET SW1
CITY OF WESTMINSTER

# HOW THE UNITED KINGDOM IS GOVERNED

## The British Constitution

In this chapter there is information about:

### Government

- The system of government

- The monarchy

- The electoral system

- Political parties

- Being a citizen

- Voting

- Contacting your MP

- The UK in Europe and the world

- The European Union

- The Commonwealth

- The United Nations

As a constitutional democracy, the United Kingdom is governed by a wide range of institutions, many of which provide checks on each other's powers. Most of these institutions are of long standing: they include the monarchy, Parliament (consisting of the House of Commons and the House of Lords), the office of Prime Minister, the Cabinet, the judiciary, the police, the civil service, and the institutions of local government. More recently, devolved administrations have been set up for Scotland, Wales and Northern Ireland. Together, these formal institutions, laws and conventions form the British Constitution. Some people would argue that the roles of other less formal institutions, such as the media and pressure groups, should also be seen as part of the Constitution.

The British Constitution is not written down in any single document, as are the constitutions of many other countries. This is mainly because the United Kingdom has never had a lasting revolution, like America or France, so our most important institutions have been in existence for hundreds of years. Some people believe that there should be a single document, but others believe that an unwritten constitution allows more scope for institutions to adapt to meet changing circumstances and public expectations.

## The monarchy

Queen Elizabeth II is the Head of State of the United Kingdom. She is also the monarch or Head of State for many countries in the Commonwealth. The UK, like Denmark, the Netherlands, Norway, Spain and Sweden, has a constitutional monarchy. This means that the king or queen does not rule the country, but appoints the government which the people have chosen in democratic elections. Although the queen or king can advise, warn and encourage the Prime Minister, the decisions on government policies are made by the Prime Minister and Cabinet.

The Queen has reigned since her father's death in 1952. Prince Charles, the Prince of Wales, her oldest son, is the heir to the throne.

The Queen has important ceremonial roles such as the opening of the new parliamentary session each year. On this occasion the Queen makes a speech that summarises the government's policies for the year ahead.

## Government

The system of government in the United Kingdom is a parliamentary democracy. The UK is divided into 646 parliamentary constituencies and at least every five years voters in each constituency elect their Member of Parliament (MP) in a general election. All of the elected MPs form the House of Commons. Most MPs belong to a political party and the party with the largest number of MPs forms the government.

The law that requires new elections to Parliament to be held at least every five years is so fundamental that no government has sought to change it. A Bill to change it is the only one to which the House of Lords must give its consent.

Some people argue that the power of Parliament is lessened because of the obligation on the United Kingdom to accept the rules of the European Union and the judgments of the European Court, but it was Parliament itself which created these obligations.

## The House of Commons

The House of Commons is the more important of the two chambers in Parliament, and its members are democratically elected. Nowadays the Prime Minister and almost all the members of the Cabinet are members of the House of Commons. The members of the House of Commons are called 'Members of Parliament' or MPs for short. Each MP represents a parliamentary constituency, or area of the country: there are 646 of these. MPs have a number of different responsibilities. They represent everyone in their constituency, they help to create new laws, they scrutinise and comment on what the government is doing, and they debate important national issues.

## Elections

There must be a general election to elect MPs at least every five years, though they may be held sooner if the Prime Minister so decides. If an MP dies or resigns, there will be another election, called a by-election, in his or her constituency. MPs are elected through a system called 'first past the post'. In each constituency, the candidate who gets the most votes is elected. The government is then formed by the party which wins the majority of constituencies.

## The Whips

The Whips are a small group of MPs appointed by their party leaders. They are responsible for discipline in their party and making sure MPs attend the House of Commons to vote. The Chief Whip often attends Cabinet or Shadow Cabinet meetings and arranges the schedule of proceedings in the House of Commons with the Speaker.

## European parliamentary elections

Elections for the European Parliament are also held every five years. There are 78 seats for representatives from the UK in the European Parliament and elected members are called Members of the European Parliament (MEPs). Elections to the European Parliament use a system of proportional representation, whereby seats are allocated to each party in proportion to the total votes it won.

## The House of Lords

Members of the House of Lords, known as peers, are not elected and do not represent a constituency. The role and membership of the House of Lords have recently undergone big changes. Until 1958 all peers were either 'hereditary', meaning that their titles were inherited, senior judges, or bishops of the Church of England. Since 1958 the Prime Minister has had the power to appoint peers just for their own lifetime. These peers, known as Life Peers, have usually had a distinguished career in politics, business, law or some other profession. This means that debates in the House of Lords often draw on more specialist knowledge than is available to members of the House of Commons. Life Peers are appointed by the Queen on the advice of the Prime Minister, but they include people nominated by the leaders of the other main parties and by an independent Appointments Commission for non-party peers.

In the last few years the hereditary peers have lost the automatic right to attend the House of Lords, although they are allowed to elect a few of their number to represent them.

While the House of Lords is usually the less important of the two chambers of Parliament, it is more independent of the government. It can suggest amendments or propose new laws, which are then discussed by the House of Commons. The House of Lords can become very important if the majority of its members will not agree to pass a law for which the House of Commons has voted. The House of Commons has powers to overrule the House of Lords, but these are very rarely used.

## The Prime Minister

The Prime Minister (PM) is the leader of the political party in power. He or she appoints the members of the Cabinet and has control over many important public appointments. The official home of the Prime Minister is 10 Downing Street, in central London, near the Houses of Parliament; he or she also has a country house not far from London called Chequers. The Prime Minister can be changed if the MPs in the governing party decide to do so, or if he or she wishes to resign. More usually, the Prime Minister resigns when his or her party is defeated in a general election.

## The Cabinet

The Prime Minister appoints about 20 senior MPs to become ministers in charge of departments. These include the Chancellor of the Exchequer, responsible for the economy, the Home Secretary, responsible for law, order and immigration, the Foreign Secretary, and ministers (called 'Secretaries of State') for education, health and defence. The Lord Chancellor, who is the minister responsible for legal affairs, is also a member of the Cabinet but sat in the House of Lords rather than the House of Commons. Following legislation passed in 2005, it is now possible for the Lord Chancellor to sit in the Commons. These ministers form the Cabinet, a small committee which usually meets weekly and makes important decisions about government policy which often then have to be debated or approved by Parliament.

## The Opposition

The second largest party in the House of Commons is called the Opposition. The Leader of the Opposition is the person who hopes to become Prime Minister if his or her party wins the next general election. The Leader of the Opposition leads his or her party in pointing out the government's failures and weaknesses; one important opportunity to do this is at Prime Minister's Questions which takes place every week while Parliament is sitting. The Leader of the Opposition also appoints senior Opposition MPs to lead the criticism of government ministers, and together they form the Shadow Cabinet.

## The Speaker

Debates in the House of Commons are chaired by the Speaker, the chief officer of the House of Commons. The Speaker is politically neutral. He or she is an MP, elected by fellow MPs to keep order during political debates and to make sure the rules are followed. This includes making sure the Opposition has a guaranteed amount of time

to debate issues it chooses. The Speaker also represents Parliament at ceremonial occasions.

## The party system

Under the British system of parliamentary democracy, anyone can stand for election as an MP but they are unlikely to win an election unless they have been nominated to represent one of the major political parties. These are the Labour Party, the Conservative Party, the Liberal Democrats, or one of the parties representing Scottish, Welsh, or Northern Irish interests. There are just a few MPs who do not represent any of the main political parties and are called 'independents'. The main political parties actively seek members among ordinary voters to join their debates, contribute to their costs, and help at elections for Parliament or for local government; they have branches in most constituencies and they hold policy-making conferences every year.

## Pressure and lobby groups

Pressure and lobby groups are organisations that try to influence government policy. They play a very important role in politics. There are many pressure groups in the UK. They may represent economic interests (such as the Confederation of British Industry, the Consumers' Association, or the trade unions) or views on particular subjects (e.g. Greenpeace or Liberty). The general public is more likely to support pressure groups than join a political party.

## The civil service

Civil servants are managers and administrators who carry out government policy. They have to be politically neutral and professional, regardless of which political party is in power. Although civil servants have to follow the policies of the elected government, they can warn ministers if they think a policy is impractical or not in the public interest. Before a general election takes place, top civil servants study the Opposition party's policies closely in case they need to be ready to serve a new government with different aims and policies.

## Devolved administration

In order to give people in Wales and Scotland more control of matters that directly affect them, in 1997 the government began a programme of devolving power from central government. Since 1999 there has been a Welsh Assembly, a Scottish Parliament and, periodically, a Northern Ireland Assembly. Although policy and laws governing defence, foreign affairs, taxation and social security all remain under central UK government control, many other public services now come under the control of the devolved administrations in Wales and Scotland.

Both the Scottish Parliament and Welsh Assembly have been set up using forms of proportional representation which ensures that each party gets a number of seats in proportion to the number of votes they receive. Similarly, proportional representation is used in Northern Ireland in order to ensure 'power sharing' between the Unionist majority (mainly Protestant) and the substantial (mainly Catholic) minority aligned to Irish nationalist parties. A different form of proportional representation is used for elections to the European Parliament.

## The Welsh Assembly Government

The National Assembly for Wales, or Welsh Assembly Government (WAG), is situated in Cardiff, the capital city of Wales. It has 60 Assembly Members (AMs) and elections are held every four years. Members can speak in either Welsh or English and all its publications are in both languages. The Assembly has the power to make decisions on important matters such as education policy, the environment, health services, transport and local government, and to pass laws for Wales on these matters within a statutory framework set out by the UK Parliament at Westminster.

## The Parliament of Scotland

A long campaign in Scotland for more independence and democratic control led to the formation in 1999 of the Parliament of Scotland, which sits in Edinburgh, the capital city of Scotland.

There are 129 Members of the Scottish Parliament (MSPs), elected by a form of proportional representation. This has led to the sharing of power in Scotland between the Labour and Liberal Democrat parties. The Scottish Parliament can pass legislation for Scotland on all matters that are not specifically reserved to the UK Parliament. The matters on which the Scottish Parliament can legislate include civil and criminal law, health, education, planning and the raising of additional taxes.

## The Northern Ireland Assembly

A Northern Ireland Parliament was established in 1922 when Ireland was divided, but it was abolished in 1972 shortly after the Troubles broke out in 1969 (see chapter 1).

Soon after the end of the Troubles, the Northern Ireland Assembly was established with a power-sharing agreement which distributes ministerial offices among the main parties. The Assembly has 108 elected members known as MLAs (Members of the Legislative Assembly). Decision-making powers devolved to Northern Ireland include education, agriculture, the environment, health and social services in Northern Ireland.

The UK government kept the power to suspend the Northern Ireland Assembly if the political leaders no longer agreed to work together or if the Assembly was not working in the interests of the people of Northern Ireland. This has happened several times and the Assembly is currently suspended (2006). This means that the elected assembly members do not have power to pass bills or make decisions.

## Local government

Towns, cities and rural areas in the UK are governed by democratically elected councils, often called local authorities. Some areas have both district and county councils which have different functions, although most larger towns and cities will have a single local authority. Many councils representing towns and cities appoint a mayor who is the ceremonial leader of the council but in some towns a mayor is appointed to be the effective leader of the administration. London has 33 local authorities, with the Greater London Authority and the Mayor of London co-ordinating policies across the capital. Local authorities are required to provide 'mandatory services' in their area. These services include education, housing, social services, passenger transport, the fire service, rubbish collection, planning, environmental health and libraries.

Most of the money for the local authority services comes from the government through taxes. Only about 20% is funded locally through 'council tax', a local tax set by councils to help pay for local services. It applies to all domestic properties, including houses, bungalows, flats, maisonettes, mobile homes or houseboats, whether owned or rented.

Local elections for councillors are held in May every year. Many candidates stand for council election as members of a political party.

## The judiciary

In the UK the laws made by Parliament are the highest authority. But often important questions arise about how the laws are to be interpreted in particular cases. It is the task of the judges (who are together called 'the judiciary') to interpret the law, and the government may not interfere with their role. Often the actions of the government are claimed to be illegal and, if the judges agree, then the government must either change its policies or ask Parliament to change the law. This has become all the more important in recent years, as the judges now have the task of applying the Human Rights Act (see chapter 7). If they find that a public body is not respecting a person's human rights, they may order that body to change its practices and to pay compensation, if appropriate. If the judges believe that an Act of Parliament is incompatible with the Human Rights Act, they cannot change it themselves but they can ask Parliament to consider doing so.

Judges cannot, however, decide whether people are guilty or innocent of serious crimes. When someone is accused of a serious crime, a jury will decide whether he or she is innocent or guilty and, if guilty, the judge will decide on the penalty. For less important crimes, a magistrate will decide on guilt and on any penalty.

## The police

The police service is organised locally, with one police service for each county or group of counties. The largest force is the Metropolitan Police, which serves London and is based at New Scotland Yard. Northern Ireland as a whole is served by the Police Service for Northern Ireland (PSNI). The police have 'operational independence', which means that the government cannot instruct them on what to do in any particular case. But the powers of the police are limited by the law and their finances are controlled by the government and by police authorities made up of councillors and magistrates. The Independent Police Complaints Commission (or, in Northern Ireland, the Police Ombudsman) investigates serious complaints against the police.

## Non-departmental public bodies (quangos)

Non-departmental public bodies, also known as quangos, are independent organisations that carry out functions on behalf of the public which it would be inappropriate to place under the political control of a Cabinet minister. There are many hundreds of these bodies, carrying out a wide variety of public duties. Appointments to these bodies are usually made by ministers, but they must do so in an open and fair way.

## The role of the media

Proceedings in Parliament are broadcast on digital television and published in official reports such as Hansard, which is available in large libraries and on the internet: www.parliament.uk. Most people, however, get information about political issues and events from newspapers (often called the press), television and radio.

The UK has a free press, meaning that what is written in newspapers is free from government control. Newspaper owners and editors hold strong political opinions and run campaigns to try and influence government policy and public opinion. As a result it is sometimes difficult to distinguish fact from opinion in newspaper coverage.

By law, radio and television coverage of the political parties at election periods must be balanced and so equal time has to be given to rival viewpoints. But broadcasters are free to interview politicians in a tough and lively way.

## Who can vote?

The United Kingdom has had a fully democratic system since 1928, when women were allowed to vote at 21, the same age as men. The present voting age of 18 was set in 1969, and (with a few exceptions such as convicted prisoners) all UK-born and naturalised citizens have full civic rights, including the right to vote and do jury service.

Citizens of the UK, the Commonwealth and the Irish Republic (if resident in the UK) can vote in all public elections. Citizens of EU states who are resident in the UK can vote in all elections except national parliamentary (general) elections.

In order to vote in a parliamentary, local or European election, you must have your name on the register of electors, known as the electoral register. If you are eligible to vote, you can register by contacting your local council election registration office. If you don't know what your local authority is,  you can find out by telephoning the Local Government Association (LGA) information line

on 020 7664 3131 between 9am and 5pm, Monday to Friday. You will have to tell them your postcode or your full address and they will be able to give you the name of your local authority. You can also get voter registration forms in English, Welsh and some other languages on the internet: www.electoralcommission.org.uk

The electoral register is updated every year in September or October. An electoral registration form is sent to every household and it has to be completed and returned, with the names of everyone who is resident in the household and eligible to vote on 15 October.

In Northern Ireland a different system operates. This is called individual registration and all those entitled to vote must complete their own registration form. Once registered, you can stay on the register provided your personal details do not change. For more information telephone the Electoral Office for Northern Ireland on 028 9044 6688.

By law, each local authority has to make its electoral register available for anyone to look at, although this now has to be supervised. The register is kept at each local electoral registration office (or council office in England and Wales). It is also possible to see the register at some public buildings such as libraries.

## Standing for office

Most citizens of the United Kingdom, the Irish Republic or the Commonwealth aged 18 or over can stand for public office. There are some exceptions and these include members of the armed forces, civil servants and people found guilty of certain criminal offences. Members of the House of Lords may not stand for election to the House of Commons but are eligible for all other public offices.

To become a local councillor, a candidate must have a local connection with the area through work, being on the electoral register, or through renting or owning land or property.

## Contacting elected members

All elected members have a duty to serve and represent their constituents. You can get contact details for all your representatives and their parties from your local library. Assembly members, MSPs, MPs and MEPs are also listed in the phone book and Yellow Pages. You can contact MPs by letter or phone at their constituency office or their office in the House of Commons: The House of Commons, Westminster, London SW1A 0AA, or telephone: 020 7729 3000. Many Assembly Members, MSPs, MPs and MEPs hold regular local 'surgeries'. These are often advertised in the local paper and constituents can go and talk about issues in person. You can find out the name of your local MP and get in touch with them by fax through the website: www.writetothem.com. This service is free.

## How to visit Parliament and the Devolved Administrations

- The public can listen to debates in the Palace of Westminster from public galleries in both the House of Commons and the House of Lords. You can either write to your local MP in advance to ask for tickets or you can queue on the day at the public entrance. Entrance is free. Sometimes there are long queues for the House of Commons and you may have to wait for at least one or two hours. It is usually easier to get into the House of Lords. You can find further information on the UK Parliament website: www.parliament.uk

- In Northern Ireland, elected members, known as MLAs, meet in the Northern Ireland Assembly at Stormont, in Belfast. The Northern Ireland Assembly is presently suspended. There are two ways to arrange a visit to Stormont. You can either contact the Education Service (details on the Northern Ireland Assembly website: www.niassembly.gov.uk) or contact an MLA

- In Scotland, the elected members, called MSPs, meet in the Scottish Parliament at Holyrood in Edinburgh (for more information see: www.scottish.parliament.uk). You can get information, book tickets or arrange tours through the visitor services. You can write to them at The Scottish Parliament, Edinburgh, EH99 1SP, or telephone 0131 348 5200, or email sp.bookings@scottish.parliament.uk

- In Wales, the elected members, known as AMs, meet in the Welsh Assembly in the Senedd in Cardiff Bay (for more information see www.wales.gov.uk). You can book guided tours or seats in the public galleries for the Welsh Assembly. To make a booking, telephone the Assembly booking line on 029 2089 8477 or email: assembly.booking@wales.gsi.gov.uk

**Check that you understand:**

- The role of the monarchy

- How Parliament works, and the difference between the House of Commons and the House of Lords

- How often general elections are held

- Where the official residence of the Prime Minister is

- The role of the Cabinet and who is in it

- The nature of the UK Constitution

- The job of the Opposition, the Leader of the Opposition and the Shadow Cabinet

- The difference between 'first past the post' and proportional representation

- The form of electoral systems in the devolved administrations in Northern Ireland, Scotland and Wales

- The rights and duties of British citizens, including naturalised citizens

- How the judiciary, police and local authorities work

- What non-departmental public bodies are

# The UK in Europe and the world

## The Commonwealth

The Commonwealth is an association of countries, most of which were once part of the British Empire, though a few countries that were not in the Empire have also joined it.

### Commonwealth members

| | | |
|---|---|---|
| Antigua and Barbuda | Kenya | Samoa |
| Australia | Kiribati | Seychelles |
| The Bahamas | Lesotho | Sierra Leone |
| Bangladesh | Malawi | Singapore |
| Barbados | Malaysia | Solomon Islands |
| Belize | Maldives | South Africa |
| Botswana | Malta | Sri Lanka |
| Brunei Darussalam | Mauritius | Swaziland |
| Cameroon | Mozambique | Tonga |
| Canada | Namibia | Trinidad and Tobago |
| Cyprus | Nauru* | Tuvalu |
| Dominica | New Zealand | Uganda |
| Fiji Islands | Nigeria | United Kingdom |
| The Gambia | Pakistan | United Republic of Tanzania |
| Ghana | Papua New Guinea | Vanuatu |
| Grenada | St Kitts and Nevis | Zambia |
| Guyana | St Lucia | |
| India | St Vincent and | |
| Jamaica | the Grenadines | *Nauru is a Special Member. |

The Queen is the head of the Commonwealth, which currently has 53 member states. Membership is voluntary and the Commonwealth has no power over its members although it can suspend membership. The Commonwealth aims to promote democracy, good government and to eradicate poverty.

## The European Union (EU)

The European Union (EU), originally called the European Economic Community (EEC), was set up by six Western European countries who signed the Treaty of Rome on 25 March 1957. One of the main reasons for doing this was the belief that co-operation between states would reduce the likelihood of another war in Europe. Originally the UK decided not to join this group and only became part of the European Union in 1973. In 2004 ten new member countries joined the EU, with a further two in 2006 making a total of 27 member countries.

One of the main aims of the EU today is for member states to function as a single market. Most of the countries of the EU have a shared currency, the euro, but the UK has decided to retain its own currency unless the British people choose to accept the euro in a referendum. Citizens of an EU member state have the right to travel to and work in any EU country if they have a valid passport or identity card. This right can be restricted on the grounds of public health, public order and public security. The right to work is also sometimes restricted for citizens of countries that have joined the EU recently.

The Council of the European Union (usually called the Council of Ministers) is effectively the governing body of the EU. It is made up of government ministers from each country in the EU and, together with the European Parliament, is the legislative body of the EU. The Council of Ministers passes EU law on the recommendations of the European Commission and the European Parliament and takes the most important decisions about how the EU is run. The European Commission is based in Brussels, the capital city of Belgium. It is the civil service of the EU and drafts proposals for new EU policies and laws and administers its funding programmes.

The European Parliament meets in Strasbourg, in north-eastern France, and in Brussels. Each country elects members, called Members of the European Parliament (MEPs), every five years. The European Parliament examines decisions made by the European Council and the European Commission, and it has the power to refuse agreement to European laws proposed by the Commission and to check on the spending of EU funds.

European Union law is legally binding in the UK and all the other member states. European laws, called directives, regulations or framework decisions, have made a lot of difference to people's rights in the UK, particularly at work. For example, there are EU directives about the procedures for making workers redundant, and regulations that limit the number of hours people can be made to work.

## The Council of Europe

The Council of Europe was created in 1949 and the UK was one of the founder members. Most of the countries of Europe are members. It has no power to make laws but draws up conventions and charters which focus on human rights, democracy, education, the environment, health and culture. The most important of these is the European Convention on Human Rights; all member states are bound by this Convention and a member state which persistently refuses to obey the Convention may be expelled from the Council of Europe.

## The United Nations (UN)

The UK is a member of the United Nations (UN), an international organisation to which over 190 countries now belong. The UN was set up after the Second World War and aims to prevent war and promote international peace and security. There are 15 members on the UN Security Council, which recommends action by the UN when there are international crises and threats to peace. The UK is one of the five permanent members. Three very important agreements produced by the UN are the Universal Declaration of Human Rights, the Convention on the Elimination of All Forms of Discrimination against Women, and the UN Convention on the Rights of the Child. Although none of these has the force of law, they are widely used in political debate and legal cases to reinforce the law and to assess the behaviour of countries.

### Check that you understand:

- The differences between the Council of Europe, the European Union, the European Commission and the European Parliament

- The UK is a member of the Council of Europe and the European Union

- The EU aims to become a single market and it is administered by a Council of Ministers of governments of member states

- Subject to some restrictions, EU citizens may travel to and work in any EU country

- The roles of the UN and the Commonwealth

# Chapter 5

# EVERYDAY NEEDS

## Housing

In this chapter there is
information about:

- Housing

- Services in and for
  the home

- Money and credit

- Health

- Pregnancy and care of
  young children

- Education

- Leisure

- Travel and transport

- Identity documents

### Buying a home

Two-thirds of people in the UK own their own home. Most other people rent houses, flats or rooms.

### Mortgages

People who buy their own home usually pay for it with a mortgage, a special loan from a bank or building society. This loan is paid back, with interest, over a long period of time, usually 25 years. You can get information about mortgages from a bank or building society. Some banks can also give information about Islamic (Sharia) mortgages.

If you are having problems paying your mortgage repayments, you can get help and advice (see **Help** on page 74). It is important to speak to your bank or building society as soon as you can.

### Estate agents

If you wish to buy a home, usually the first place to start is an estate agent. In Scotland the process is different and you should go first to a solicitor. Estate agents represent the person selling their house or flat. They arrange for buyers to visit homes that are for sale. There are estate agents in all towns and cities and they usually have websites where they advertise the homes for sale. You can also find details about homes for sale on the internet and in national and local newspapers.

## Making an offer

In the UK, except in Scotland, when you find a home you wish to buy you have to make an offer to the seller. You usually do this through an estate agent or solicitor. Many people offer a lower price than the seller is asking. Your first offer must be 'subject to contract' so that you can withdraw if there are reasons why you cannot complete the purchase. In Scotland the seller sets a price and buyers make offers over that amount. The agreement becomes legally binding earlier than it does elsewhere in the UK.

## Solicitor and surveyor

It is important that a solicitor helps you through the process of buying a house or flat. When you make an offer on a property, the solicitor will carry out a number of legal checks on the property, the seller and the local area. The solicitor will provide the legal agreements necessary for you to buy the property. The bank or building society that is providing you with your mortgage will also carry out checks on the house or flat you wish to buy. These are done by a surveyor. The buyer does not usually see the result of this survey, so the buyer often asks a second surveyor to check the house as well. In Scotland the survey is carried out before an offer is made, to help people decide how much they want to bid for the property.

## Rented accommodation

It is possible to rent accommodation from the local authority (the council), from a housing association or from private property owners called landlords.

## The local authority

Most local authorities (or councils) provide housing. This is often called 'council housing'. In Northern Ireland social housing is provided by the Northern Ireland Housing Executive (www.nihe.co.uk). In Scotland you can find information on social housing at: www.sfha.co.uk. Everyone is entitled to apply for council accommodation. To apply you must put your name on the council register or list. This is available from the housing department at the local authority. You are then assessed according to your needs. This is done through a system of points. You get more points if you have priority needs, for example if you are homeless and have children or chronic ill health.

It is important to note that in many areas of the UK there is a shortage of council accommodation, and that some people have to wait a very long time for a house or flat.

## Housing associations

Housing associations are independent not-for-profit organisations which provide housing for rent. In some areas they have taken over the administration of local authority housing. They also run schemes called shared ownership, which help people buy part of a house or flat if they cannot afford to buy all of it at once. There are usually waiting lists for homes owned by housing associations.

## Privately rented accommodation

Many people rent houses or flats privately, from landlords. Information about private accommodation can be found in local newspapers, notice boards, estate agents and letting agents.

## Tenancy agreement

When you rent a house or flat privately you sign a tenancy agreement, or lease. This explains the conditions or 'rules' you must follow while renting the property. This agreement must be checked very carefully to avoid problems later. The agreement also contains a list of any furniture or fittings in the property. This is called an inventory. Before you sign the agreement, check the details and keep it safe during your tenancy.

## Deposit and rent

You will probably be asked to give the landlord a deposit at the beginning of your tenancy. This is to cover the cost of any damage. It is usually equal to one month's rent. The landlord must return this money to you at the end of your tenancy, unless you have caused damage to the property.

Your rent is fixed with your landlord at the beginning of the tenancy. The landlord cannot raise the rent without your agreement.

If you have a low income or are unemployed you may be able to claim Housing Benefit (see **Help**) to help you pay your rent.

## Renewing and ending a tenancy

Your tenancy agreement will be for a fixed period of time, often six months. After this time the tenancy can be ended or, if both tenant and landlord agree, renewed. If you end the tenancy before the fixed time, you usually have to pay the rent for the agreed full period of the tenancy.

A landlord cannot force a tenant to leave. If a landlord wishes a tenant to leave they must follow the correct procedures. These vary according to the type of tenancy. It is a criminal offence for a landlord to use threats or violence against a tenant or to force them to leave without an order from court.

## Discrimination

It is unlawful for a landlord to discriminate against someone looking for accommodation because of their sex, race, nationality, or ethnic group, or because they are disabled, unless the landlord or a close relative of the landlord is sharing the accommodation.

## Homelessness

If you are homeless you should go for help to the local authority (or, in Northern Ireland, the Housing Executive). They have a legal duty to offer help and advice, but will not offer you a place to live unless you have priority need (see above) and have a connection with the area, such as work or family. You must also show that you have not made yourself intentionally homeless.

## Help

If you are homeless or have problems with your landlord, help can be found from the following:

- The housing department of the local authority will give advice on homelessness and on Housing Benefit as well as deal with problems you may have in council-owned property

- The Citizens Advice Bureau will give advice on all types of housing problems. There may also be a housing advice centre in your neighbourhood

- Shelter is a housing charity which runs a 24-hour helpline on 0808 800 4444, or visit www.shelternet.org.uk

- Help with the cost of moving and setting up home may be available from the Social Fund. This is run by the Department for Work and Pensions (DWP). It provides grants and loans such as the Community Care Grant for people setting up home after being homeless or after they have been in prison or other institutions. Other loans are available for people who have had an emergency such as flooding. Information about these is available at the Citizens Advice Bureau or Jobcentre Plus.

# Services in and for the home

## Water

Water is supplied to all homes in the UK. The charge for this is called the water rates. When you move in to a new home (bought or rented), you should receive a letter telling you the name of the company responsible for supplying your water. The water rates may be paid in one payment (a lump sum) or in instalments, usually monthly. If you receive Housing Benefit, you should check to see if this covers the water rates. The cost of the water usually depends on the size of your property, but some homes have a water meter which tells you exactly how much water you have used. In Northern Ireland water is currently (2006) included in the domestic rates (see **Council tax** on page 76), although this may change in future.

## Electricity and gas

All properties in the UK have electricity supplied at 240 volts. Most homes also have gas. When you move into a new home or leave an old one, you should make a note of the electricity and gas meter readings. If you have an urgent problem with your gas, electricity or water supply, you can ring a 24-hour helpline. This can be found on your bill, in the Yellow Pages or in the phone book.

## Gas and electricity suppliers

It is possible to choose between different gas and electricity suppliers. These have different prices and different terms and conditions. Get advice before you sign a contract with a new supplier. To find out which company supplies your gas, telephone Transco on 0870 608 1524

To find out which company supplies your electricity, telephone Energywatch on 0845 906 0708 or visit: www.energywatch.org.uk. Energywatch can also give you advice on changing your supplier of electricity or gas.

## Telephone

Most homes already have a telephone line (called a land line). If you need a new line, telephone BT on 150 442, or contact a cable company. Many companies offer land line, mobile telephone and broadband internet services. You can get advice about prices or about changing your company from Ofcom at: www.ofcom.org.uk. You can call from public payphones using cash, pre-paid phonecards or credit or debit cards. Calls made from hotels and hostels are usually more expensive. Dial 999 or 112 for emergency calls for police, fire or ambulance service. These calls are free. Do not use these numbers if it is not a real emergency; you can always find the local numbers for these services in the phone book.

## Bills

Information on how to pay for water, gas, electricity and the telephone is found on the back of each bill. If you have a bank account you can pay your bills by standing order or direct debit. Most companies operate a budget scheme which allows you to pay a fixed sum every month. If you do not pay a bill, the service can be cut off. To get a service reconnected, you have to pay another charge.

## Refuse collection

Refuse is also called waste, or rubbish. The local authority collects the waste regularly, usually on the same day of each week. Waste must be put outside in a particular place to get collected. In some parts of the country the waste is put into plastic bags, in others it is put into bins with wheels. In many places you must recycle your rubbish, separating paper, glass, metal or plastic from the other rubbish. Large objects which you want to throw away, such as a bed, a wardrobe or a fridge, need to be collected separately. Contact the local authority to arrange this. If you have a business, such as a factory or a shop, you must make special arrangements with the local authority for your waste to be collected. It is a criminal offence to dump rubbish anywhere.

## Council Tax

Local government services, such as education, police, roads, refuse collection and libraries, are paid for partly by grants from the government and partly by Council Tax (see **Local government** on page 48). In Northern Ireland there is a system of domestic rates instead of the Council Tax. The amount of Council Tax you pay depends on the size and value of your house or flat (dwelling). You must register to pay Council Tax when you move into a new property, either as the owner or the tenant. You can pay the tax in one payment, in two instalments, or in ten instalments (from April to January).

If only one person lives in the flat or house, you get a 25% reduction on your Council Tax. (This does not apply in Northern Ireland). You may also get a reduction if someone in the property has a disability. People on a low income or who receive benefits such as Income Support or Jobseeker's Allowance can get Council Tax Benefit. You can get advice on this from the local authority or the Citizens Advice Bureau.

## Buildings and household insurance

If you buy a home with a mortgage, you must insure the building against fire, theft and accidental damage. The landlord should arrange insurance for rented buildings. It is also wise to insure your possessions against theft or damage. There are many companies that provide insurance.

## Neighbours

If you live in rented accommodation, you will have a tenancy agreement. This explains all the conditions of your tenancy. It will probably include information on what to do if you have problems with your housing. Occasionally, there may be problems with your neighbours. If you do have problems with your neighbours, they can usually be solved by speaking to them first. If you cannot solve the problem, speak to your landlord, local authority or housing association. Keep a record of the problems in case you have to show exactly what the problems are and when they started. Neighbours who cause a very serious nuisance may be taken to court and can be evicted from their home.

There are several mediation organisations which help neighbours to solve their disputes without having to go to court. Mediators talk to both sides and try to find a solution acceptable to both. You can get details of mediation organisations from the local authority, Citizens Advice, and Mediation UK on 0117 904 6661 or visit: www.mediationuk.co.uk.

### Check that you understand:

- The process for buying and renting accommodation

- Where to get advice about accommodation and moving

- The role of an estate agent

- Housing priorities for local authorities

- Where to get help if you are homeless

- How you can pay for the water you use at home

- Recycling your waste

- What Council Tax pays for

- What to do if you have problems with your neighbours

# Money and credit

Bank notes in the UK come in denominations (values) of £5, £10, £20 and £50. Northern Ireland and Scotland have their own bank notes which are valid everywhere in the UK, though sometimes people may not realise this and may not wish to accept them.

## The euro

In January 2002 twelve European Union (EU) states adopted the euro as their common currency. The UK government decided not to adopt the euro at that time, and has said it will only do so if the British people vote for the euro in a referendum. The euro does circulate to some extent in Northern Ireland, particularly in the towns near the border with Ireland.

## Foreign currency

You can get or change foreign currency at banks, building societies, large post offices and exchange shops or bureaux de change. You might have to order some currencies in advance. The exchange rates vary and you should check for the best deal.

## Banks and building societies

Most adults in the UK have a bank or building society account. Many large national banks or building societies have branches in towns and cities throughout the UK. It is worth checking the different types of account each one offers. Many employers pay salaries directly into a bank or building society account. There are many banks and building societies to choose from. To open an account, you need to show documents to prove your identity, such as a passport, immigration document or driving licence. You also need to show something with your address on it like a tenancy agreement or household bill. It is also possible to open bank accounts in some supermarkets or on the internet.

## Cash and debit cards

Cash cards allow you to use cash machines to withdraw money from your account. For this you need a Personal Identification Number (PIN) which you must keep secret.

A debit card allows you to pay for things without using cash. You must have enough money in your account to cover what you buy. If you lose your cash card or debit card you must inform the bank immediately.

## Credit and store cards

Credit cards can be used to buy things in shops, on the telephone and over the internet. A store card is like a credit card but used only in a specific shop. Credit and store cards do not draw money from your bank account, but you will be sent a bill every month. If you do not pay the total amount on the bill, you are charged interest. Although credit and store cards are useful, the interest is usually very high and many people fall into debt this way. If you lose your credit or store cards you must inform the company immediately.

## Credit and loans

People in the UK often borrow money from banks and other organisations to pay for things like household goods, cars and holidays. This is more common in the UK than in many other countries. You must be very sure of the terms and conditions when you decide to take out a loan. You can get advice on loans from the Citizens Advice Bureau if you are uncertain.

## Being refused credit

Banks and other organisations use different information about you to make a decision about a loan, such as your occupation, address, salary and previous credit record. If you apply for a loan you might be refused. If this happens, you have the right to ask the reason why.

## Credit unions

Credit unions are financial co-operatives owned and controlled by their members. The members pool their savings and then make loans from this pool. Interest rates in credit unions are usually lower than banks and building societies. There are credit unions in many cities and towns. To find the nearest credit union contact the Association of British Credit Unions (ABCUL) on: www.abcul.coop.

## Insurance

As well as insuring their property and possessions (see above), many people insure their credit cards and mobile phones. They also buy insurance when they travel abroad in case they lose their luggage or need medical treatment. Insurance is compulsory if you have a car or motorcycle. You can usually arrange insurance directly with an insurance company, or you can use a broker who will help you get the best deal.

## Social security

**jobcentreplus**

Including Jobcentres and
social security offices

The UK has a system of social security which pays welfare
benefits to people who do not have enough money to
live on. Benefits are usually available for the sick and
disabled, older people, the unemployed and those on
low incomes. People who do not have legal rights of
residence (or 'settlement') in the UK cannot usually receive
benefits. Arrangements for paying and receiving benefits
are complex because they have to cover people in many
different situations. Guides to benefits are available from
Jobcentre Plus offices, local libraries, post offices and the
Citizens Advice Bureau.

**Check that you understand:**

- What you need to open a bank or building
society account

- What debit, credit and store cards are

- What a credit union is

- What insurance is

- How to get help with benefits and problems
with debt

# Health

Healthcare in the UK is organised under the National Health Service (NHS). The NHS began in 1948, and is one of the largest organisations in Europe. It provides all residents with free healthcare and treatment.

## Finding a doctor

Family doctors are called General Practitioners (GPs) and they work in surgeries. GPs often work together in a group practice. This is sometimes called a Primary Health Care Centre.

Your GP is responsible for organising the health treatment you receive. Treatment can be for physical and mental illnesses. If you need to see a specialist, you must go to your GP first. Your GP will then refer you to a specialist in a hospital. Your GP can also refer you for specialist treatment if you have special needs.

You can get a list of local GPs from libraries, post offices, the tourist information office, the Citizens Advice Bureau, the local Health Authority and from the following websites:

www.nhs.uk/ for health practitioners in England; www.wales.nhs.uk/directory.cfm for health practitioners in Wales;

www.n-i.nhs.uk for health practitioners in Northern Ireland; www.show.scot.nhs.uk/findnearest/healthservices in Scotland. You can also ask neighbours and friends for the name of their local doctor.

You can attend a hospital without a GP's letter only in the case of an emergency. If you have an emergency you should go to the Accident and Emergency (A & E) department of the nearest hospital.

## Registering with a GP

You should look for a GP as soon as you move to a new area. You should not wait until you are ill. The health centre, or surgery, will tell you what you need to do to register. Usually you must have a medical card. If you do not have one, the GP's receptionist should give you a form to send to the local health authority. They will then send you a medical card.

Before you register you should check the surgery can offer what you need. For example, you might need a woman GP, or maternity services. Sometimes GPs have many patients and are unable to accept new ones. If you cannot find a GP, you can ask your local health authority to help you find one.

## Using your doctor

All patients registering with a GP are entitled to a free health check. Appointments to see the GP can be made by phone or in person. Sometimes you might have to wait several days before you can see a doctor. If you need immediate medical attention ask for an urgent appointment. You should go to the GP's surgery a few minutes before the appointment. If you cannot attend or do not need the appointment any more, you must let the surgery know. The GP needs patients to answer all questions as fully as possible in order to find out what is wrong. Everything you tell the GP is completely confidential and cannot be passed on to anyone else without your permission. If you do not understand something, ask for clarification. If you have difficulties with English, bring someone who can help you, or ask the receptionist for an interpreter. This must be done when you make the appointment. If you have asked for an interpreter, it is important that you keep your appointment because this service is expensive.

In exceptional circumstances, GPs can visit patients at home but they always give priority to people who are unable to travel. If you call the GP outside normal working hours, you will have to answer several questions about your situation. This is to assess how serious your case is. You will then be told if a doctor can come to your home. You might be advised to go to the nearest A & E department.

## Charges

Treatment from the GP is free but you have to pay a charge for your medicines and for certain services, such as vaccinations for travel abroad. If the GP decides you need to take medicine you will be given a prescription. You must take this to a pharmacy (chemist).

## Prescriptions

Prescriptions are free for anyone who is:

- under 16 years of age (under 25 in Wales)

- under 19 and in full-time education

- aged 60 or over

- pregnant or with a baby under 12 months old

- suffering from a specified medical condition

- receiving Income Support, Jobseekers' Allowance, Working Families or Disabilities Tax Credit.

## Feeling unwell

If you or your child feels unwell you have the following options:

For information or advice:

- ask your local pharmacist (chemist). The pharmacy can give advice on medicines and some illnesses and conditions that are not serious

- speak to a nurse by phoning NHS Direct on 0845 46 47

- use the NHS Direct website, NHS Direct Online: www. nhsdirect.nhs.uk

To see a doctor or nurse:

- make an appointment to see your GP or a nurse working in the surgery

- visit an NHS walk-in centre.

For urgent medical treatment

- contact your GP

- go to your nearest hospital with an Accident and Emergency department

- call 999 for an ambulance. Calls are free. ONLY use this service for a real emergency.

NHS Direct is a 24-hour telephone service which provides information on particular health conditions. Telephone: 0845 46 47. You may ask for an interpreter for advice in your own language. In Scotland, NHS24 at: www.nhs24.com or telephone 08454 24 24 24.

NHS Direct Online is a website providing information about health services and several medical conditions and treatments: www.nhsdirect.nhs.uk

NHS walk-in centres provide treatment for minor injuries and illnesses seven days a week. You do not need an appointment. For details of your nearest centre call NHS Direct or visit the NHS website at: www.nhs.uk (for Northern Ireland www.n-i.nhs.uk) and click on 'local NHS services'.

## Going into hospital

If you need minor tests at a hospital, you will probably attend the Outpatients department. If your treatment takes several hours, you will go into hospital as a day patient. If you need to stay overnight, you will go into hospital as an in-patient.

You should take personal belongings with you, such as a towel, night clothes, things for washing, and a dressing gown. You will receive all your meals while you are an in-patient. If you need advice about going into hospital, contact Customer Services or the Patient Advice and Liaison Service (PALS) at the hospital where you will receive treatment.

## Dentists

You can get the name of a dentist by asking at the local library, at the Citizens Advice Bureau and through NHS Direct. Most people have to pay for dental treatment. Some dentists work for the NHS and some are private. NHS dentists charge less than private dentists, but some have two sets of charges, both NHS and private. A dentist should explain your treatment and the charges before the treatment begins.

Free dental treatment is available to

- people under 18 (in Wales people under 25 and over 60)

- pregnant women and women with babies under 12 months old

- people on income support, Jobseekers' Allowance or Pension Credit Guarantee

## Opticians

Most people have to pay for sight tests and glasses, except children, people over 60, people with certain eye conditions and people receiving certain benefits. In Scotland, eye tests are free.

## Pregnancy and care of young children

If you are pregnant you will receive regular ante-natal care. This is available from your local hospital, local health centre or from special antenatal clinics. You will receive support from a GP and from a midwife. Midwives work in hospitals or health centres. Some GPs do not provide maternity services so you may wish to look for another GP during your pregnancy. In the UK women usually have their babies in hospital, especially if it is their first baby. It is common for the father to attend the birth, but only if the mother wants him to be there.

A short time after you have your child, you will begin regular contact with a health visitor. She or he is a qualified nurse and can advise you about caring for your baby. The first visits will be in your home, but after that you might meet the health visitor at a clinic. You can ask advice from your health visitor until your child is five years old. In most towns and cities there are mother and toddler groups or playgroups for small children. These often take place at local churches and community centres. You might be able to send your child to a nursery school (see **Going to school** on page 86).

## Information on pregnancy

You can get information on maternity and ante-natal services in your area from your local health authority, a health visitor or your GP. The number of your health authority will be in the phone book.

The Family Planning Association (FPA) gives advice on contraception and sexual health. The FPA's helpline is 0845 310 1334, or: www.fpa.org.uk

The National Childbirth Trust gives information and support in pregnancy, childbirth and early parenthood: www.nctpregnancyandbabycare.com

## Registering a birth

Your must register your baby with the Registrar of Births, Marriages and Deaths (Register Office) within six weeks of the birth. The address of your local Register Office is in the phone book. If the parents are married, either the mother or father can register the birth. If they are not married, only the mother can register the birth. If the parents are not married but want both names on the child's birth certificate, both mother and father must be present when they register their baby.

## Education

### Going to school

Education in the UK is free and compulsory for all children between the ages of 5 and 16 (4 to 16 in Northern Ireland). The education system varies in England, Scotland, Wales and Northern Ireland.

The child's parent or guardian is responsible for making sure their child goes to school, arrives on time and attends for the whole school year. If they do not do this, the parent or guardian may be prosecuted.

Some areas of the country offer free nursery education for children over the age of 3. In most parts of the UK, compulsory education is divided into two stages, primary and secondary. In some places there is a middle-school system. In England and Wales the primary stage lasts from 5 to 11, in Scotland from 5 to 12 and in Northern Ireland from 4 to 11. The secondary stage lasts until the age of 16. At that age young people can choose to leave school or to continue with their education until they are 17 or 18.

Details of local schools are available from your local education authority office or website. The addresses and phone numbers of local education authorities are in the phone book.

**Check that you understand:**

- How to find and register with a GP

- What to do if you feel unwell

- How to find other services such as dentists and opticians

- When it is possible to attend A & E without a doctor's letter

- Who can get free prescriptions

- When you should phone 999 or 112

- What NHS Direct can do

- Who can give health advice and treatment when you are pregnant and after you have a baby

- How to register a birth

## Primary schools

These are usually schools where both boys and girls learn together and are usually close to a child's home. Children tend to be with the same group and teacher all day. Schools encourage parents to help their children with learning, particularly with reading and writing.

## Secondary schools

At age 11 (12 in Scotland) children go to secondary school. This might normally be the school nearest their home, but parents in England and Wales are allowed to express a preference for a different school. In some areas, getting a secondary school place in a preferred school can be difficult, and parents often apply to several schools in order to make sure their child gets offered a place. In Northern Ireland many schools select children through a test taken at the age of 11.

If the preferred school has enough places, the child will be offered a place. If there are not enough places, children will be offered places according to the school's admission arrangements. Admission arrangements vary from area to area.

Secondary schools are larger than primary schools. Most are mixed sex, although there are single sex schools in some areas. Your local education authority will give you information on schools in your area. It will also tell you which schools have spaces and give you information about why some children will be given places when only a few are available and why other children might not. It will also tell you how to apply for a secondary school place.

## Costs

Education at state schools in the UK is free, but parents have to pay for school uniforms and sports wear. There are sometimes extra charges for music lessons and for school outings. Parents on low incomes can get help with costs, and with the cost of school meals. You can get advice on this from the local education authority or the Citizens Advice Bureau.

## Church and other faith schools

Some primary and secondary schools in the UK are linked to the Church of England or the Roman Catholic Church. These are called 'faith schools'. In some areas there are Muslim, Jewish and Sikh schools. In Northern Ireland, some schools are called Integrated Schools. These schools aim to bring children of different religions together. Information on faith schools is available from your local education authority.

## Independent schools

Independent schools are private schools. They are not run or paid for by the state. Independent secondary schools are also sometimes called public schools. There are about 2,500 independent schools in the UK. About 8% of children go to these schools. At independent schools parents must pay the full cost of their child's education. Some independent schools offer scholarships which pay some or all of the costs of the child's education.

## The school curriculum

All state, primary and secondary schools in England, Wales and Northern Ireland follow the National Curriculum. This covers English, maths, science, design and technology, information and communication technology (ICT), history, geography, modern foreign languages, art and design, music, physical education (PE) and citizenship. In Wales, children learn Welsh.

In some primary schools in Wales, all the lessons are taught in Welsh. In Scotland, pupils follow a broad curriculum informed by national guidance. Schools must, by law, provide religious education (RE) to all pupils. Parents are allowed to withdraw their children from these lessons. RE lessons have a Christian basis but children also learn about the other major religions.

## Assessment

In England, the curriculum is divided into four stages, called Key Stages. After each stage children are tested. They take Key Stage tests (also called SATs) at ages 7, 11 and 14. At 16 they usually take the General Certificates of Secondary Education (GCSEs) in several subjects, although some schools also offer other qualifications. At 18, young people who have stayed at school do AGCEs (Advanced GCE levels) often just called A levels.

In Wales, schools follow the Welsh National Curriculum but have abolished national tests for children at age 7 and 11. There are also plans in Wales to stop testing children at 14. Teachers in Wales still have to assess and report on their pupils' progress and achievements at 7 and 11.

In Scotland, the curriculum is divided into two phases. The first phase is from 5 to 14. There are six levels in this phase, levels A to F. There are no tests for whole groups during this time. Teachers test individual children when they are ready. From 14 to 16, young people do Standard Grade. After 16 they can study at Intermediate, Higher or Advanced level. In Scotland there will soon be a single curriculum for all pupils from age 3 to age 18. This is called A Curriculum for Excellence. More information can be found at: www.acurriculumforexcellencescotland.gov.uk.

## Help with English

If your child's main language is not English, the school may arrange for extra language support from an EAL (English Additional Language) specialist teacher.

## Careers education

All children get careers advice from the age of 14. Advice is also available from Connexions, a national service for young people: telephone 080 800 13219 or: www.connexions-direct.com in England. In Wales, Careers Wales offers advice to children from the age of 11. For further information visit: www.careerswales.com or telephone 0800 100 900.

In Scotland, Careers Scotland provides information, services and support to all ages and stages. For further information visit: www.careers-scotland.org.uk or telephone 0845 8 502 502.

## Parents and schools

Many parents are involved with their child's school. A number of places on a school's governing body are reserved for parents. The governing body decides how the school is run and administered and produces reports on the progress of the school from year to year. In Scotland, parents can be members of school boards or parent councils.

Schools must be open 190 days a year. Term dates are decided by the governing body or by the local education authority. Children must attend the whole school year. Schools expect parents and guardians to inform them if their child is going to be absent from school. All schools ask parents to sign a home-school agreement. This is a list of things that both the school and the parent or guardian agree to do to ensure a good education for the child. All parents receive a report every year on their child's progress. They also have the chance to go to the school to talk to their child's teachers.

## Further education and adult education

At 16, young people can leave school or stay on to do A levels (Higher grades in Scotland) in preparation for university. Some young people go to their local further education (FE) college to improve their exam grades or to get new qualifications for a career. Most courses are free up to the age of 19. Young people from families with low incomes can get financial help with their studies when they leave school at 16. This is called the Education Maintenance Allowance (EMA). Information about this is available at your local college or at: www.dfes.gov.uk.

Further education colleges also offer courses to adults over the age of 18. These include courses for people wishing to improve their skills in English. These courses are called ESOL (English for Speakers of Other Languages). There are also courses for English speakers who need to improve their literacy and numeracy and for people who need to learn new skills for employment. ESOL courses are also available in community centres and training centres. There is sometimes a waiting list for ESOL courses because demand is high. In England and Wales, ESOL, literacy and numeracy courses are also called Skills for Life courses. You can get information at your local college or local library or from learndirect on 0800 100 900.

Many people join other adult education classes to learn a new skill or hobby and to meet new people. Classes are very varied and range from sports to learning a musical instrument or a new language. Details are usually available from your local library, college or adult education centre.

## University

More young people go to university now than in the past. Many go after A levels (or Higher grades in Scotland) at age 18 but it is also possible to go to university later in life. At present, most students in England, Wales and Northern Ireland have to pay towards the cost of their tuition fees and to pay for their living expenses. In Scotland there are no tuition fees but after students finish university they pay back some of the cost of their education in a payment called an endowment. At present, universities can charge up to £3,000 per year for their tuition fees, but students do not have to pay anything towards their fees before or during their studies. The government pays their tuition fees and then charges for them when a student starts working after university. Some families on low incomes receive help with their children's tuition fees. This is called a grant. The universities also give help, in the form of bursaries. Most students get a low-interest student loan from a bank. This pays for their living costs while they are at university. When a student finishes university and starts working, he or she must pay back the loan.

## Leisure

### Information

Information about theatre, cinema, music and exhibitions is found in local newspapers, local libraries and tourist information offices. Many museums and art galleries are free.

### Film, video and DVD

Films in the UK have a system to show if they are suitable for children. This is called the classification system. If a child is below the age of the classification, they should not watch the film at a cinema or on DVD. All films receive a classification, as follows:

**U** (Universal): suitable for anyone aged 4 years and over

**PG** (parental guidance): suitable for everyone but some parts of the film might be unsuitable for children. Their parents should decide.

**12** or **12a**: children under 12 are not allowed to see or rent the film unless they are with an adult.

**15**: children under 15 are not allowed to see or rent the film.

**18**: no one under 18 is allowed to see or rent the film.

**R18**: no one under 18 is allowed to see the film, which is only available in specially licensed cinemas.

## Television and radio

Anyone in the UK with a television (TV), DVD or video recorder, computer or any device which is used for watching or recording TV programmes must be covered by a valid television licence. One licence covers all of the equipment at one address, but people who rent different rooms in a shared house must each buy a separate licence.

A colour TV licence currently costs £131.50 (2006) and lasts for 12 months. People aged 75, or over can apply for a free TV licence. Blind people can claim a 50% discount on their TV licence. You risk prosecution and a fine if you watch TV but are not covered by a TV licence. There are many ways to buy a TV licence including from local Pay Point outlets or on-line at: www.tvlicensing.co.uk. It is also possible to pay for the licence in instalments. For more information telephone 0870 576 3763 or write to TV Licensing, Bristol BS98 1TL.

## Sports, clubs and societies

Information about local clubs and societies can usually be found at local libraries or through your local authority. For information about sports you should ask in the local leisure centre. Libraries and leisure centres often organise activities for children during the school holidays.

## Places of interest

The UK has a large network of public footpaths in the countryside. Many parts of the countryside and places of interest are kept open by the National Trust. This is a charity that works to preserve important buildings and countryside in the UK. Information about National Trust buildings and areas open to the public is available on: www.nationaltrust.org.uk

## Pubs and night clubs

Public houses, or pubs, are an important part of social life in the UK. To drink alcohol in a pub you must be 18 or over. People under 18 are not allowed to buy alcohol in a supermarket or in an off-licence either. The landlord of the pub may allow people of 14 to come into the pub but they are not allowed to drink. At 16, people can drink wine or beer with a meal in a hotel or restaurant.

Pubs are usually open during the day and until 11pm. If a pub wants to stay open later, it must apply for a special licence. Night clubs open and close later than pubs.

## Travel and Transport

### Betting and gambling

People under 18 are not allowed into betting shops or gambling clubs. There is a National Lottery for which draws, with large prizes, are made every week. You can enter by buying a ticket or a scratch card. People under 16 are not allowed to buy a lottery ticket or scratch card.

### Pets

Many people in the UK have pets such as cats and dogs. It is against the law to treat a pet cruelly or to neglect it. All dogs in public places must wear a collar showing the name and address of the owner. The owner is responsible for keeping the dog under control and for cleaning up after the animal in a public place. Vaccinations and medical treatment for animals are available from veterinary surgeons (vets). If you cannot afford to pay a vet, you can go to a charity called the PDSA (People's Dispensary for Sick Animals). To find your nearest branch, visit: www.pdsa.org.uk.

### Trains, buses and coaches

For information about trains telephone the National Rail Enquiry Service: 08457 48 49 50, or visit: www.nationalrail.co.uk For trains in Northern Ireland, phone Translink on 028 90 66 66 30 or visit: www.translink.co.uk. For information about local bus times phone 0870 608 250. For information on coaches, telephone National Express on 08705 80 80 80, or visit: www.nationalexpress.com For coaches in Scotland, telephone Scottish Citylink on 08705 50 50 50 or visit: www.citylink.co.uk For Northern Ireland, visit: www.translink.co.uk

Usually, tickets for trains and underground systems such as the London Underground must be bought before you get on the train. The fare varies according to the day and time you wish to travel. Travelling in the rush hour is always more expensive. Discount tickets are available for families, people aged 60 and over, disabled people, students and people under 26. Ask at your local train station for details. Failure to buy a ticket may result in a penalty.

### Taxis

To operate legally, all taxis and minicabs must be licensed and display a licence plate. Taxis and cabs with no licence are not insured for fare-paying passengers and are not always safe. Women should not use unlicensed minicabs.

## Driving

You must be at least 17 to drive a car or motorcycle, 18 to drive a medium-sized lorry, and 21 to drive a large lorry or bus. To drive a lorry, minibus or bus with more than eight passenger seats, you must have a special licence.

## The driving licence

You must have a driving licence to drive on public roads. To get a driving licence you must pass a test. There are many driving schools where you can learn with the help of a qualified instructor.

You get a full driving licence in three stages:

**1**. Apply for a provisional licence. You need this licence while you are learning to drive. With this you are allowed to drive a motorcycle up to 125cc or a car. You must put L plates on the vehicle, or D plates in Wales. Learner drivers cannot drive on a motorway. If you drive a car, you must be with someone who is over 21 and who has had a full licence for over three years. You can get an application form for a provisional licence from a post office.

**2**. Pass a written theory test.

**3**. Pass a practical driving test.

Drivers may use their licence until they are 70. After that the licence is valid for three years at a time.

In Northern Ireland, a newly-qualified driver must display an R-Plate (for registered driver) for one year after passing the test.

## Overseas licences

If your driving licence is from a country in the European Union (EU), Iceland, Liechtenstein or Norway, you can drive in the UK for as long as your licence is valid.

If you have a licence from a country outside the EU, you may use it in the UK for up to 12 months. During this time you must get a UK provisional driving licence and pass both the UK theory and practical driving tests, or you will not be able to drive after 12 months.

## Insurance

It is a criminal offence to have a car without proper motor insurance. Drivers without insurance can receive very high fines. It is also illegal to allow someone to use your car if they are not insured to drive it.

## Road tax and MOT

You must also pay a tax to drive your car on the roads. This is called road tax. Your vehicle must have a road tax disc which shows you have paid. You can buy this at the post office. If you do not pay the road tax, your vehicle may be clamped or towed away.

If your vehicle is over three years old, you must take it every year for a Ministry of Transport (MOT) test. You can do this at an approved garage. The garage will give you an MOT certificate when your car passes the test. It is an offence not to have an MOT certificate. If you do not have an MOT certificate, your insurance will not be valid.

## Safety

Everyone in a vehicle should wear a seat belt. Children under 12 years of age may need a special booster seat. Motorcyclists and their passengers must wear a crash helmet (this law does not apply to Sikh men if they are wearing a turban). It is illegal to drive while holding a mobile phone.

## Speed limits

For cars and motorcycles the speed limits are:

- 30 miles per hour (mph) in built-up areas, unless a sign shows a different limit

- 60 mph on single carriageways

- 70 mph on motorways and dual carriageways.

Speed limits are lower for buses, lorries and cars pulling caravans.

It is illegal to drive when you are over the alcohol limit or drunk. The police can stop you and give you a test to see how much alcohol you have in your body. This is called a breathalyser test. If a driver has more than the permitted amount of alcohol (called being 'over the limit') or refuses to take the test, he or she will be arrested. People who drink and drive can expect to be disqualified from driving for a long period.

## Accidents

If you are involved in a road accident:

- don't drive away without stopping - this is a criminal offence

- call the police and ambulance on 999 or 112 if someone is injured

- get the names, addresses, vehicle registration numbers and insurance details of the other drivers

- give your details to the other drivers or passengers and to the police

- make a note of everything that happened and contact your insurance company as soon as possible.

Note that if you admit the accident was your fault, the insurance company may refuse to pay. It is better to wait until the insurance company decides for itself whose fault the accident was.

## Identity documents

At present, UK citizens do not have to carry identity (ID) cards. The government is, however, making plans to introduce them in the next few years.

## Proving your identity

You may have to prove your identity at different times, such as when you open a bank account, rent accommodation, enrol for a college course, hire a car, apply for benefits such as housing benefit, or apply for a marriage certificate. Different organisations may ask for different documents as proof of identity. These can include:

- official documents from the Home Office showing your immigration status

- a certificate of identity

- a passport or travel document

- a National Insurance (NI) number card

- a provisional or full driving licence

- a recent gas, electricity or phone bill showing your name and address

- a rent or benefits book.

**Check that you understand:**

- How films are classified

- Why you need a television licence

- The rules about the selling and drinking of alcohol

- How to get a driving licence

- What you need to do to be allowed to drive a vehicle in the UK

- What you should do if you have an accident

- When you might have to prove your identity, and how you can do it

# Chapter 6: EMPLOYMENT

## Looking for work

In this chapter there is information about:

- Looking for work and applying for jobs

- Training and volunteering

- Equal rights and discrimination

- Rights and responsibilities at work

- Working for yourself

- Childcare and children at work

If you are looking for work, or you are thinking of changing your job, there are a number of ways you can find out about work opportunities. The Home Office provides guidance on who is allowed to work in the UK. Not everyone in the UK is allowed to work and some people need work permits, so it is important to check your status before taking up work. Also, employers have to check that anyone they employ is legally entitled to work in the UK. For more information and guidance, see the Home Office website 'Working in the UK': www.workingintheuk.gov.uk

Jobs are usually advertised in local and national newspapers, at the local Jobcentre and in employment agencies. You can find the address and telephone number of your local Jobcentre under Jobcentre Plus in the phone book or see: www.jobcentreplus.gov.uk Some jobs are advertised on supermarket notice boards and in shop windows. These jobs are usually part-time and the wages are often quite low. If there are particular companies you would like to work for, you can look for vacancies on their websites.

Jobcentre Plus is run by a government department - the Department for Work and Pensions. Trained staff give advice and help in finding and applying for jobs as well claiming benefits. They can also arrange for interpreters. Their website www.jobcentreplus.gov.uk lists vacancies and training opportunities and gives general information

on benefits. There is also a low-cost telephone service
- Jobseeker Direct, 0845 60 60 234. This is open 9a.m. to
6.p.m. on weekdays and 9 a.m. to 1 p.m. on Saturdays.

## Qualifications

Applicants for some jobs need special training or
qualifications. If you have qualifications from another
country, you can find out how they compare with
qualifications in the UK at the National Academic
Recognition Information Centre (NARIC),
www.naric.org.uk

For further information contact UK NARIC, ECCTIS Ltd,
Oriel House, Oriel Road, Cheltenham Glos, GL50 1XP,
telephone: 0870 990 4088, email: info@naric.org.uk

## Applications

Interviews for lower paid and local jobs can often be
arranged by telephone or in person. For many jobs you
need to fill in an application form or send a copy of your
curriculum vitae (CV) with a covering letter or letter
of application.

A covering letter is usually a short letter attached to a
completed application form, while a letter of application
gives more detailed information on why you are applying
for the job and why you think you are suitable. Your CV
gives specific details on your education, qualifications,
previous employment, skills and interests. It is important
to type any letters and your CV on a computer or word
processor as this improves your chance of being called for
an interview.

Employers often ask for the names and addresses of one
or two referees. These are people such as your current or
previous employer or college tutor. Referees need to know
you well and to agree to write a short report or reference
on your suitability for the job. Personal friends or members
of your family are not normally acceptable as referees.

## Interviews

In job descriptions and interviews, employers should
give full details of what the job involves, including the
pay, holidays and working conditions. If you need more
information about any of these, you can ask questions
in the interview. In fact, asking some questions in the
interview shows you are interested and can improve your
chance of getting the job.

When you are applying for a job and during the interview,
it is important to be honest about your qualifications and
experience. If an employer later finds out that you gave
incorrect information, you might lose your job.

## Criminal record

For some jobs, particularly if the work involves working with children or vulnerable people, the employer will ask for your permission to do a criminal record check. You can get more information on this from the Home Office Criminal Records Bureau (CRB) information line, telephone 0870 90 90 811. In Scotland, contact Disclosure Scotland: www.disclosurescotland.co.uk Helpline: 0870 609 6006.

## Training

Taking up training helps people improve their qualifications for work. Some training may be offered at work or you can do courses from home or at your local college. This includes English language training. You can get more information from your local library and college or from websites such as www.worktrain.gov.uk and www.learndirect.co.uk. Learndirect offers a range of online training courses at centres across the country. There are charges for courses but you can do free starter or taster sessions. You can get more information from their free information and advice line: 0800 100 900.

## Volunteering and work experience

Some people do voluntary work and this can be a good way to support your local community and organisations which depend on volunteers. It also provides useful experience that can help with future job applications. Your local library will have information about volunteering opportunities.

**Check that you understand:**

- The Home Office provides guidance on who is entitled to work in the UK

- NARIC can advise on how qualifications from overseas compare with qualifications form the UK

- What CVs are

- Who can be a referee

- What happens if any of the information you have given is untrue

- When you need a CRB check

- Where you can find out about training opportunities and job seeking

- Benefits of volunteering in terms of work experience and community involvement

# Equal rights and discrimination

You can also get information and advice from websites such as: www.do-it.org.uk, www.volunteering.org.uk and www.justdosomething.net It is against the law for employers to discriminate against someone at work. This means that a person should not be refused work, training or promotion or treated less favourably because of their:

- sex

- nationality, race, colour or ethnic group

- disability

- religion

- sexual orientation

- age.

In Northern Ireland, the law also bans discrimination on grounds of religious belief or political opinion.

The law also says that men and women who do the same job, or work of equal value, should receive equal pay. Almost all the laws protecting people at work apply equally to people doing part-time or full-time jobs.

There are, however, a small number of jobs where discrimination laws do not apply. For example, discrimination is not against the law when the job involves working for someone in their own home.

You can get more information about the law and racial discrimination from the Commission for Racial Equality. The Equal Opportunities Commission can help with sex discrimination issues and the Disability Rights Commission deals with disability issues. Each of these organisations offers advice and information and can, in some cases, support individuals. From October 2007 their functions will be brought together in a new Commission for Equality and Human Rights. You can get more information about the laws protecting people at work from the Citizens Advice Bureau website: www.adviceguide.org.uk

In Northern Ireland, the Equality Commission provides information and advice in respect of all forms of unlawful discrimination.

The Commission for Racial Equality, St Dunstan's House, 201-211 Borough High Street, London, SE1 1GZ, telephone: 020 7939 000, fax: 020 7939 0001, www.cre.gov.uk

The Equal Opportunities Commission, Arndale House, Arndale Centre, Manchester M4 3EQ, telephone: 0845 601 5901, fax: 0161 838 8312, www.eoc.org.uk

The Disability Rights Commission, DRC Helpline, FREEPOST MID02164, Stratford upon Avon CV37 9BR, telephone: 08457 622 633, fax: 08457 778 878, www.drc.org.uk

The Equality Commission for Northern Ireland, Equality House, 7-9 Shaftesbury Square, Belfast BT2 7DP, telephone: 028 90 500600, www.equalityni.org

## Sexual harassment

Sexual harassment can take different forms. This includes:

- indecent remarks

- comments about the way you look that make you feel uncomfortable or humiliated

- comments or questions about your sex life

- inappropriate touching or sexual demands

- bullying behaviour or being treated in a way that is rude, hostile, degrading or humiliating because of your sex.

Men and women can be victims of sexual harassment at work. If this happens to you, tell a friend, colleague or trade union representative and ask the person harassing you to stop. It is a good idea to keep a written record of what happened, the days and times when it happened and who else may have seen or heard the harassment. If the problem continues, report the person to your employer or trade union. Employers are responsible for the behaviour of their employees while they are at work. They should treat complaints of sexual harassment very seriously and take effective action to deal with the problem. If you are not satisfied with your employer's response, you can ask for advice and support from the Equal Opportunities Commission, your trade union or the Citizens Advice Bureau.

# At work

Both employers and employees have legal responsibilities at work. Employers have to pay employees for the work that they do, treat them fairly and take responsible care for their health and safety. Employees should do their work with reasonable skill and care and follow all reasonable instructions. They should not damage their employer's business.

## A written contract or statement

Within two months of starting a new job, your employer should give you a written contract or statement with all the details and conditions for your work. This should include your responsibilities, pay, working hours, holidays, sick pay and pension. It should also include the period of notice that both you and your employer should give for the employment to end. The contract or written statement is an important document and is very useful if there is ever a disagreement about your work, pay or conditions.

## Pay, hours and holidays

Your pay is agreed between you and your employer. There is a minimum wage in the UK that is a legal right for every employed person above compulsory school leaving age. The compulsory school leaving age is 16, but the time in

the school year when 16-year-olds can leave school in England and Wales is different from that in Scotland and Northern Ireland.

There are different minimum wage rates for different age groups. From October 2006 the rates are as follows:

- for workers aged 22 and above - £5.35 an hour

- for 18-21 year olds - £4.45 an hour

- for 16-17 year olds - £3.30 an hour.

Employers who pay their workers less than this are breaking the law. You can get more information from the Central Office of Information Directgov website, www.direct.gov.uk which has a wide range of public service information. Alternatively, you can telephone the National Minimum Wage Helpline, telephone: 0845 600 0678.

Your contract or statement will show the number of hours you are expected to work. Your employer might ask you if you can work more hours than this and it is your decision whether or not you do. Your employer cannot require you to work more hours than the hours agreed on your contract.

If you need to be absent from work, for example if you are ill or you have a medical appointment, it is important to tell your employer as soon as you can in advance. Most employees who are 16 or over are entitled to at least four weeks' paid holiday every year. This includes time for national holidays (see chapter 3). Your employer must give you a pay slip, or a similar written statement, each time you are paid. This must show exactly how much money has been taken off for tax and National Insurance contributions.

## Tax

For most people, tax is automatically taken from their earnings by the employer and paid directly to HM Revenue and Customs, the government department responsible for collecting taxes. If you are self-employed, you need to pay your own tax (see page 109). Money raised from income tax pays for government services such as roads, education, police and the armed forces. Occasionally HM Revenue and Customs sends out tax return forms which ask for full financial details. If you receive one, it is important to complete it and return the form as soon as possible. You can get help and advice from the HM Revenue and Customs self-assessment helpline, on: 0845 300 45 55.

## National Insurance

Almost everybody in the UK who is in paid work, including self-employed people, must pay National Insurance (NI) contributions. Money raised from NI contributions is used to pay contributory benefits such as the State Retirement Pension and helps fund the National Health Service. Employees have their NI contributions deducted from their pay by their employer every week or month. People who are self-employed need to pay NI contributions themselves: Class 2 contributions, either by direct debit or every three months, and Class 4 contributions on the profits from their trade or business. Class 4 contributions are paid alongside their income tax. Anyone who does not pay enough NI contributions will not be able to receive certain benefits, such as Jobseeker's Allowance or Maternity Pay, and may not receive a full state retirement pension.

## Getting a National Insurance number

Just before their 16th birthday, all young people in the UK are sent a National Insurance number. This is a unique number for each person and it tracks their National Insurance contributions.

Refugees whose asylum applications have been successful have the same rights to work as any other UK citizen and to receive a National Insurance number. People who have applied for asylum and have not received a positive decision do not usually have permission to work and so do not get a National Insurance number.

You need a National Insurance number when you start work. If you do not have a National Insurance number, you can apply for one through Jobcentre Plus or your local Social Security Office. It is a good idea to make an appointment by telephone and ask which documents you need to take with you. You usually need to show your birth certificate, passport and Home Office documents allowing you to stay in the country. If you need information about registering for a National Insurance number, you can telephone the National Insurance Registrations Helpline on 0845 91 57006 or 0845 91 55670.

## Pensions

Everyone in the UK who has paid enough National Insurance contributions will get a State Pension when they retire. The State Pension age for men is currently 65 years of age and for women it is 60, but the State Pension age for women will increase to 65 in stages between 2010 and 2020. You can find full details of the State Pension scheme on the State Pension website: www.thepensionservice.gov.uk or you can phone the Pension Service Helpline: 0845 60 60 265.

In addition to a State Pension, many people also receive a pension through their work and some also pay into a personal pension plan too. It is very important to get good advice about pensions. The Pensions Advisory Service gives free and confidential advice on occupational and personal pensions. Their helpline telephone number is 0845 601 2923 and their website address is www.opas.org.uk. Independent financial advisers can also give advice but you usually have to pay a fee for this service. You can find local financial advisers in the Yellow Pages and Thomson local guides or on the internet at www.unbiased.co.uk

## Health and safety

Employers have a legal duty to make sure the workplace is safe. Employees also have a legal duty to follow safety regulations and to work safely and responsibly. If you are worried about health and safety at your workplace, talk to your supervisor, manager or trade union representative. You need to follow the right procedures and your employer must not dismiss you or treat you unfairly for raising a concern.

## Trade unions

Trade unions are organisations that aim to improve the pay and working conditions of their members. They also give their members advice and support on problems at work. You can choose whether to join a trade union or not and your employer cannot dismiss you or treat you unfairly for being a union member.

You can find details of trade unions in the UK, the benefits they offer to members and useful information on rights at work on the Trades Union Congress (TUC) website, www.tuc.org.uk

## Problems at work

If you have problems of any kind at work, speak to your supervisor, manager, trade union representative or someone else with responsibility as soon as possible. If you need to take any action, it is a good idea to get advice first. If you are a member of a trade union, your representative will help. You can also contact your local Citizens Advice Bureau (CAB) or Law Centre. The national Advisory, Conciliation and Arbitration Service (ACAS) website, www.acas.org.uk gives information on your rights at work. ACAS also offers a national helpline, telephone: 08457 47 47 47.

## Losing your job and unfair dismissal

An employee can be dismissed immediately for serious misconduct at work. Anyone who cannot do their job properly, or is unacceptably late or absent from work, should be given a warning by their employer. If their work, punctuality or attendance does not improve, the employer can give them notice to leave their job.

It is against the law for employers to dismiss someone from work unfairly. If this happens to you, or life at work is made so difficult that you feel you have to leave, you may be able to get compensation if you take your case to an Employment Tribunal. This is a court which specialises in employment matters. You normally only have three months to make a complaint.

If you are dismissed from your job, it is important to get advice on your case as soon as possible. You can ask for advice and information on your legal rights and the best action to take from your trade union representative, a solicitor, a Law Centre or the Citizen's Advice Bureau.

## Redundancy

If you lose your job because the company you work for no longer needs someone to do your job, or cannot afford to employ you, you may be entitled to redundancy pay. The amount of money you receive depends on the length of time you have been employed. Again your trade union representative, a solicitor, a Law Centre or the Citizens Advice Bureau can advise you.

## Unemployment

Most people who become unemployed can claim Jobseeker's Allowance (JSA). This is currently available for men aged 18-65 and women aged 18-60 who are capable of working, available for work and trying to find work. Unemployed 16- and 17-year-olds may not be eligible for Jobseeker's Allowance but may be able to claim a Young Person's Bridging Allowance (YPBA) instead. The local Jobcentre Plus can help with claims. You can get further information from the Citizens Advice Bureau and the Jobcentre Plus website: www.jobcentreplus.gov.uk

## New Deal

New Deal is a government programme that aims to give unemployed people the help and support they need to get into work. Young people who have been unemployed for 6 months and adults who have been unemployed for 18 months are usually required to join New Deal if they wish to continue receiving benefit. There are different New Deal schemes for different age groups. You can find out more about New Deal on 0845 606 2626 or: www.newdeal.gov.uk

The government also runs work-based learning programmes which offer training to people while they are at work. People receive a wage or an allowance and can attend college for one day a week to get a new qualification.

You can find out more about the different government schemes, and the schemes in your area, from Jobcentre Plus, www.jobcentreplus.gov.uk, or your local Citizens Advice Bureau.

# Working for yourself

## Tax

Self-employed people are responsible for paying their own tax and National Insurance. They have to keep detailed records of what they earn and spend on the business and send their business accounts to HM Revenue and Customs every year. Most self-employed people use an accountant to make sure they pay the correct tax and claim all the possible tax allowances.

As soon as you become self-employed you should register yourself for tax and National Insurance by ringing the HM Revenue and Customs telephone helpline for people who are self-employed, on 0845 915 4515.

## Help and advice

Banks can give information and advice on setting up your own business and offer start-up loans, which need to be repaid with interest. Government grants and other financial support may be available. You can get details of these and advice on becoming self-employed from Business Link, a government-funded project for people starting or running a business - www.businesslink.gov.uk or telephone: 0845 600 9006.

## Working in Europe

British citizens can work in any country that is a member of the European Economic Area (EEA). In general, they have the same employment rights as a citizen of that country or state.

## Check that you understand

### Equal rights

- the categories covered by the law and exceptions

- equal job/equal pay regardless of gender

- the different commissions working to promote equal opportunities

- the grounds for sexual harassment complaints

### At work

- the importance of contracts of employment

- the minimum wage and holiday entitlement

- information that has to be provided on pay slips

### Tax

- what is deducted from your earnings and why

### Tax *continued*

- the difference between being self-employed and employed

- where to get help if you need it when filling out forms

- the purpose of National Insurance and what happens if you don't pay enough contributions

- how you can get a National Insurance number

### Pensions

- who is entitled to a pension

- what age men and women can get a pension

### Health and safety

- employer and employee obligations

- what to do if you have concerns about health and safety

## Childcare and children at work

### New mothers and fathers

Women who are expecting a baby have a legal right to time off work for antenatal care. They are also entitled to at least 26 weeks' maternity leave. These rights apply to full-time and part-time workers and it makes no difference how long the woman has worked for her employer. It is, however, important to follow the correct procedures and to give the employer enough notice about taking maternity leave. Some women may also be entitled to maternity pay but this depends on how long they have been working for their employer.

Fathers who have worked for their employer for at least 26 weeks are entitled to paternity leave, which provides up to two weeks' time off from work, with pay, when the child is born. It is important to tell your employer well in advance.

You can get advice and more information on maternity and paternity matters from the personnel officer at work, your trade union representative, your local Citizens Advice Bureau, the Citizens Advice Bureau website www.adviceguide.org.uk or the government website www.direct.gov.uk

### Trade unions

- what they are and who can join

### Losing your job

- where to go if you need advice on a problem at work

- possible reasons for dismissal

- the role of Employment Tribunals

- who can help

- the timescale for complaining

- entitlement to redundancy pay

### Self-employment

- responsibility for keeping detailed records and paying tax and national insurance

- the role of Business Link

## Childcare

It is government policy to help people with childcare responsibilities to take up work. Some employers can help with this. The ChildcareLink website www.childcarelink.gov.uk gives information about different types of childcare and registered childminders in your area, or telephone 08000 96 02 96.

### Hours and time for children at work

In the UK there are strict laws to protect children from exploitation and to make sure that work does not get in the way of their education. The earliest legal age for children to do paid work is 13, although not all local authorities allow this. There are exceptions for some types of performance work (including modelling) when younger children may be allowed to work. Any child under school leaving age (16) seeking to do paid work must apply for a licence from the local authority. Children taking part in some kinds of performances may have to obtain a medical certificate before working.

By law, children under 16 can only do light work. There are particular jobs that children are not allowed to do. These include delivering milk, selling alcohol, cigarettes or medicines, working in a kitchen or behind the counter of a chip shop, working with dangerous machinery or chemicals, or doing any other kind of work that may be harmful to their health or education.

The law sets out clear limits for the working hours and times for 13–16 year old children. Every child must have at least two consecutive weeks a year during the school holidays when they do not work. They cannot work:

- for more than 4 hours without a one hour rest break

- for more than 2 hours on any school day or a Sunday

- more than five hours (13–14 year olds) or eight hours (15–16 year olds) on Saturdays (or weekdays during school holidays)

- before 7.00am or after 7.00pm

- before the close of school hours (except in areas where local bylaws allow children to work one hour before school).

- for more than 12 hours in any school week

- for more than 25 hours a week (13–14 year olds) or 35 hours a week (15–16 year olds) during school holidays.

There is no national minimum wage for those under 16.

The local authority may withdraw a child's licence to work, for example where a child works longer hours than the law allows. The child would then be unable to continue to work. An employer may be prosecuted for illegally employing a child. A parent or carer who makes a false declaration in a child's licence application can also be prosecuted. They may also be prosecuted if they do not ensure their child receives a proper education. You can find more information on the TUC website, www.worksmart.org.uk

**Check that you understand:**

**Maternity and paternity rights**

- entitlement to maternity leave and pay for both part time and full-time workers

- paternity leave entitlement

- the importance of following the right procedures and providing sufficient notice

**Children at work**

- minimum age for starting work

- jobs that children under 16 are not allowed to do

- Maternity and paternity rights

- the maximum hours allowed

- licence and medical certificate requirements

- the local authority's role in licensing and protecting children in employment

- parents' responsibilities to ensure that children work within the law and get proper education.

Chapter 7:    # KNOWING THE LAW

## The rights and duties of a citizen

### The law

In this chapter there is information about:

- The police

- Crime and the law

- Criminal courts

- Human rights

- Marriage and divorce

- Children and young people

- Consumer protection

Every person in the UK has the right to equal treatment under the law. The law applies in the same way to everyone - regardless of who they are or where they are from.

The law can be divided into criminal and civil law. Criminal law relates to crimes, which are usually investigated by the police or some other authority and are punished by the courts. Civil law is used to settle disputes between individuals or groups.

In the UK it is a criminal offence to carry a weapon such as a gun or knife or anything that is made or adapted to cause injury to someone, even if it is for self-defence.

### Reporting a crime

In an emergency, or if you are the victim of a crime or you see a crime taking place, dial 999 or 112. The operator will ask you which service you need - police, fire, ambulance or, by the coast, the coastguard. Then you need to explain why the police are needed and where they need to go.

If the situation is NOT an emergency, you can either go to your local police station or telephone them. You can find the telephone number under 'Police' in the phone book. Some 'minor' crimes can be reported online. See www.online.police.uk for details.

## Racially and religiously motivated crime

In the UK it is a criminal offence to use abusive or insulting words in public because of someone's religion or ethnic origin. Anyone who causes harassment, alarm or distress to other people because of their religion or ethnic origin can be prosecuted and given strong penalties by the courts. If you are the victim of religious or racially motivated crime, it is important to report this to the police and they have a duty to take action. You can ask for an interview at the police station, at your home or somewhere else.

You can get further information and advice from the Race Equality Council or from your local Citizens Advice Bureau.

## Police duties

The job of the police in the UK is to:

- protect life and property

- prevent disturbances (known as keeping the peace)

- prevent and detect crime.

The police force is a public service and should help and protect everyone. You should not be afraid of reporting a crime or asking the police for help. Police officers must obey the law and they must not misuse their authority, make a false statement, be rude, abusive or commit racial discrimination. The very small numbers of police officers who are corrupt or misuse their authority are severely punished.

## Complaints

Anyone can make an official complaint against the police. To make a complaint, you can go to a police station or write to either the Chief Constable for that police force or the Independent Police Complaints Commission (in Northern Ireland, the Police Ombudsman). If it is a serious matter, it is a good idea to speak to a solicitor or to the Citizens Advice Bureau first.

## If the police ever stop you

All good citizens are expected to help the police prevent and detect crimes whenever they can. The police can stop any member of the public on foot in connection with a crime that has been committed or is about to take place. They can stop people in a vehicle at any time.

If you are stopped by the police you should give the officer your name and address. You do not need to answer any more questions, although usually people do. You can ask for the name of the officer who stopped and questioned you, the police station where he or she is based and the reason why you have been stopped.

The police can ask you to go to a police station to answer more questions and you can choose whether to go. If you go to a police station voluntarily, you are entitled to leave when you want to. If you are obstructive, rude or decide to mislead the police, you risk being arrested.

## Search

The police can stop and search anyone they think might be involved in a crime. This includes offences such as theft, burglary or possession of illegal drugs or things to be used for committing criminal damage. They can also search the vehicle of the person they stop.

Police officers do not have the power to enter and search any building they choose, but they can enter a building if they have a warrant (that is, special permission from a magistrate, in Scotland a Sheriff), or to arrest someone, to save a life or to prevent serious disturbance or damage.

You can ask for the name of the officer who has stopped you, the police station where he or she is based and the reason for their search.

## Arrest

If you are arrested and taken to a police station, a police officer will tell you the reason for your arrest.

If you have difficulty in understanding English, the police should provide an interpreter unless they think a delay in finding an interpreter might result in serious harm to a person or property.

The police should normally only interview a young person under the age of 17 if their parent or an 'appropriate adult' is present. This could be a social worker, an adult friend or a teacher.

## Information and advice

If you are arrested or detained at a police station, you are given written details of three important legal rights:

1 the right to see a solicitor

2 the right to send a message to a friend or a member of your family, telling them where you are

3 the right to look at the codes of practice - guidelines that the police should follow when searching for and collecting evidence.

This written note also includes the official police caution given to all suspects:

You do not have to say anything.
But it may harm your defence if you do not mention, when questioned, something which you later rely on in court.
Anything you do say may be given in evidence.

This caution means that the police cannot force a person to answer questions. But if a suspect does not answer questions at the police station, or in court, this can be used as evidence against him or her. The caution also states that anything a person does say to a police officer can also be used as evidence in court.

## The duty solicitor

Anyone who has been arrested or goes to a police station voluntarily is entitled to legal advice in private. This can be with a solicitor of their choice or the duty solicitor. Duty solicitors work for local firms that specialise in criminal law and offer a free consultation. Usually the advice is given in person but sometimes it may be given over the telephone.

If you have been arrested, or are being questioned about a serious offence, or you feel unsure about your legal position, you have the right not to answer questions (except to give your name and address) until you have spoken to a solicitor.

There are some differences between the court system in England and Wales and the system in Scotland and Northern Ireland.

## Magistrates' and district courts

In England, Wales and Northern Ireland most minor criminal cases are dealt with in a magistrates' court. In Scotland, minor criminal offences go to a district court.

# Criminal courts

Magistrates, also known as Justices of the Peace, hear less serious cases in magistrates' and district courts. They are members of the local community. In England and Wales they usually work unpaid and have no legal qualifications, although they do receive training. In Northern Ireland, cases are only heard by paid magistrates.

## Crown Courts and sheriff courts

In England, Wales and Northern Ireland, serious offences are tried in front of a judge and a jury in a Crown Court. In Scotland, serious cases are heard in a sheriff court with either a sheriff or a sheriff with a jury. A jury is made up of members of the public chosen at random from the local electoral register (see chapter 4). In England, Wales and Northern Ireland a jury has 12 members, and in Scotland a jury has 15 members. Everyone who is summoned to do jury service must do it unless they are not eligible, for example if they work in law enforcement, or they provide a good reason to be excused, such as ill health. The jury decides on the verdict, that is whether the defendant is innocent or guilty, and if the verdict is guilty the judge decides on the penalty.

## Youth court

If an accused person is 17 years old or younger, their case is normally heard in a youth court in front of up to three specially trained magistrates or a district judge. The most serious cases will go to a Crown Court. The parents of the young person are expected to attend the hearing. Members of the public are not allowed in youth courts and neither the name nor the photograph of the young person can be published in newspapers or used by the media. In Scotland there is a unique system called the Children's Hearings System, and Northern Ireland now has a system based on 'youth conferencing'.

## Civil courts

### County courts

Most towns and cities have a county court to deal with a wide range of civil disputes. These include people trying to get back money that is owed to them, cases involving personal injury, family matters, breaches of contract and divorce. In Scotland, all of these matters are dealt with in the sheriff court.

### The small claims procedure

The small claims procedure is an informal way of helping people to settle minor disputes without spending a lot of time and money using a solicitor. This procedure is usually used for claims of less than £5,000. The hearing is held in an ordinary room with a judge and people from both sides of the dispute sitting around a table. You can get details about the small claims procedure from your local county court (in Scotland local sheriff court), which is listed under Courts in the phone book.

## Legal advice and aid

### Solicitors

Solicitors are trained lawyers who give advice on legal matters, take action for their clients and represent their clients in court. There are solicitors' offices throughout the UK. It is important to find out which aspects of law a solicitor specialises in and to check that they have the right experience to help you with your case. Many advertise in local papers and the Yellow Pages, and the Citizens Advice Bureau can give you names of local solicitors and which areas of law they specialise in. You can also get this information from the Law Society (telephone: 020 7242 1222, www.solicitors-online.com) and the Community Legal Service (telephone: 0845 345 4345, www.clsdirect.org.uk).

### Costs

Solicitors' charges are usually based on how much time they spend on a case. It is very important to find out at the start how much a case is likely to cost and whether you are eligible for legal aid.

### Financial help or legal aid

Anyone who is questioned or charged in connection with a crime is entitled to free advice from a duty solicitor (see above) and free representation by a solicitor for their first appearance in court. It may also be possible to get help with costs for any further appearances in court, although this depends on the type of case and the income and savings of the client. A solicitor can give information and advice on this.

Solicitors can also give information on schemes to cover the cost of a solicitor's help, but not all types of case are covered by these schemes and the help available also depends on the income and savings of the client. Sometimes the costs are paid by the client on a 'no win, no fee' basis. In no win, no fee cases, the solicitor only charges the client if they win the case. It is important to check all the possible costs before agreeing to a solicitor taking a case as no win, no fee, as there are often hidden costs such as paying the costs of the other side.

## Law Centres

Most large cities have one or more Law Centres staffed by qualified lawyers. They can give legal advice and possibly take on a case. To find the address of your nearest centre, you can telephone the Law Centres Federation on 020 7387 8570 or visit: www.lawcentres.org.uk

## Other advice and information

There is a Citizens Advice Bureau in most towns and cities. They give free and confidential advice on many different types of legal problems. Their website also gives a wide range of information in English, Welsh, Bengali, Chinese, Gujarati, Punjabi and Urdu: www.adviceguide.org.uk

## Just ask!

www.clsdirect.org.uk is the website of the Community Legal Service and it gives information on a wide range of legal questions in seven languages. It can also give you details of local solicitors and places to go for advice in your area.

## For teenagers

The Young Citizen's Passport is a practical guide to everyday law written especially for the needs of young people aged 14 to 19. It is produced by the Citizenship Foundation and there are three different editions: England and Wales, Scotland and Northern Ireland. You can order a copy through a local bookshop or telephone the publishers, Hodder Murray, on 020 7837 6372.

## Victims of crime

Anyone who is the victim of a violent crime can apply to the Criminal Injuries Compensation Authority for compensation for their injuries. The crime has to be reported to the police as quickly as possible and the application for compensation must be made within two years of the crime. You can find more information on the Criminal Injuries Compensation Authority website: www.cica.gov.uk

Victims of crime can also get free help and guidance from Victim Support. You can find their telephone number in the local phone book, ring their national helpline on 845 30 30 900 or go to their website: www.victimsupport.com

**Check that you understand:**

- How the police force is organised and the responsibilities of the police

- How to report a crime

- Your rights if you are stopped and searched or arrested

- How to make a complaint about the police and get support if you are the victim of a crime

- That it is illegal to carry a weapon

- The different types of criminal and civil courts

- How to get legal advice and legal aid

# Human rights

## The Human Rights Act

All UK courts must follow the principles of the European Convention on Human Rights. These rights are set out in British law in the Human Rights Act 1998 and apply to everyone in the UK. Public bodies such as the police, schools and hospitals have to work in a way that follows the Human Rights Act.

There is more general information on the Human Rights Act on the Department of Constitutional Affairs website: www.dca.gov.uk/peoples-rights/human-rights/index.htm

In Northern Ireland there is a Human Rights Commission, which is considering whether Northern Ireland needs its own additional human rights law. It also works with its counterpart in the Republic of Ireland with the aim of achieving common standards in both parts of the island.

## Equal opportunities

For more than 30 years the law in the UK has been developed to try and make sure that people are not treated unfairly in all areas of life and work because of their sex, race, disability, sexuality or religion. In 2006 unfair age discrimination at work also became unlawful.

If you face problems with discrimination, you can get more information from the Citizens Advice Bureau or from one of the following organisations:

The Commission for Racial Equality - www.cre.gov.uk
The Equal Opportunities Commission - www.eoc.org.uk
The Disability Rights Commission - www.drc.org.uk

(These three organisations will be brought together in the Commission for Equality and Human Rights from October 2007.)

The Equality Commission for Northern Ireland - www.equalityni.org

For further information on discrimination at work, see chapter 6.

## Military service

In the UK there has been no compulsory military service since 1960.

## The Human Rights Act lists 16 basic rights (the 'Convention Rights'):

- **The right to life** - Everyone has the right for their life to be protected by the law. The state can only take someone's life in very limited circumstances, such as when a police officer acts justifiably in self-defence

- **Prohibition of torture** - No one should be tortured or punished or treated in an inhuman or degrading way

- **Prohibition of slavery and forced labour** - No one should be held in slavery or forced to work

- **The right to liberty and security** - Everyone has the right not to be detained or have their liberty taken away, unless it is within the law and the correct legal procedures are followed

- **The right to a fair trial** - Everyone has the right to a fair trial and a public hearing within a reasonable period of time. Everyone charged with a criminal offence is presumed innocent until proved guilty

- **No punishment without law** - No one should be found guilty of an offence that was not a crime at the time it was committed

- **Right to respect a person's private and family life** - Everyone has the right for their private and family life, their home and their correspondence to be respected. There should not be any interference with this unless there are very good reasons, such as state security, public safety or the prevention of a crime

- **Freedom of thought, conscience and religion** - Everyone is free to hold whatever views and beliefs they wish. Again, this right is only limited for reasons such as public safety, the protection of public order and the protection of the freedom and rights of others

- **Freedom of expression** - Everyone has the freedom to express their views. This may, however, be limited for reasons of public safety or to protect the rights of others

*continued...*

- **Freedom of assembly and association** - Everyone has the right to get together with other people in a peaceful way. This again may be limited for reasons of public safety or to protect the rights of others

- **Right to marry** - Men and women have the right to marry and start a family, but national law may put restrictions on when this may take place and with whom

- **Prohibition of discrimination** - Everyone is entitled to the rights and freedoms set out in the European Convention on Human Rights. This is regardless of their race, sex, language, religion, political opinion, national or social origin or for any other reason.

- **Protection of property** - No one should be deprived of their possessions except in the public interest, such as when the state raises taxes or confiscates goods that are unlawful or dangerous

- **The right to education** - No one should be denied the right to education

- **The right to free elections** - Elections for government must be free, fair and take place at reasonable intervals with a secret ballot

- **Prohibition of the death penalty** - No one can be condemned to death or executed

## Marriage

In order to marry, each partner must be 16 years old or older, and unmarried. Anyone who is 16 or 17 and wants to get married needs written permission from their parents. Close blood relatives are not allowed to marry each other although cousins are allowed to marry. No one can be forced to get married regardless of how strong the wishes of their family may be. Couples who have agreed to marry usually announce their engagement. In the past an engagement was seen as a legal contract but these days it is not.

A marriage ceremony can take place in a registry office, a registered place of worship or in premises that have been approved by the local authority. You can get a list of these from your local authority.

In order for a marriage ceremony to take place, couples need to get certificates from the registrar of marriages in the district(s) where they live. In order to get a certificate, the partners need to show their birth certificates or, if these are not available, their personal identity documents. If either of the partners has been married before, they need to show proof that this marriage has ended. Certificates can be collected between 21 days and 3 months before the date of the wedding.

The procedure for marriages in the Church of England is slightly different. The traditional method used by most couples is the publication of banns, which takes the same time as the civil method of getting married by certificate. The banns are published by being read aloud during the service on each of the three Sundays before the ceremony. You do not have to be a member of the church to be married there but it is usual for the couple to attend the church on at least one of the three occasions when the banns are read. You can get more details from either a religious minister who is authorised to conduct marriages or the local registrar of marriages - see Registration of births, marriages and deaths in the phone book.

In the UK, many women take their husband's surname when they get married. But there is no legal duty to do this and some women prefer to keep their own surname.

## Living together

These days, many couples in the UK live together without getting married or live together before they get married. Couples who live together without being married do not have the same legal rights as couples who are married and may face some problems if their relationship breaks up. For example, if only one partner's name is on a tenancy agreement or title deeds to a property, the other partner may have difficulty staying in a property or claiming a share in its value.

If a married person dies without making a will, their husband or wife is entitled to all or most of their possessions. But if a couple are not married and there is no will, it can be very difficult for the surviving partner to claim any of their partner's possessions.

If an unmarried couple have a child, both parents have a duty to support that child until he or she is 18 years old.

## Same-sex partnerships

Couples of the same sex can now legally register their relationship and mark this with a civil ceremony known as a civil partnership. When they do this they have similar legal rights to those of married couples.

## Divorce

A divorce cannot take place during the first year of marriage. In order for a man or a woman to apply for a divorce they must prove to a court that their marriage has 'irretrievably broken down'. In order to do this, he or she must prove one of the following things has happened:

- their partner has committed adultery

- their partner has behaved unreasonably. This can cover many things such as domestic violence, assault, or refusing to have children

- they have lived apart for two years and both want a divorce

- they have lived apart for five years and only one partner wants a divorce

- one partner has deserted the other for at least two years before the application for divorce

## Help and advice

The breakdown of a marriage can be a very difficult time for everyone involved. Family doctors can sometimes help by arranging an appointment with a family therapist. There is also a voluntary and independent organisation called Relate, which operates in England and Wales. You can find their contact details in the phone book under Relate or at www.relate.org.uk

# Children

If you are facing divorce, or if your partner has left you, it is very important to get advice about your legal position from a solicitor, particularly if you have young children or if there is disagreement over money or property.

## Domestic violence

In the UK, brutality and violence in the home is a serious crime. Anyone who is violent towards their partner - whether they are a man or a woman, married or living together - can be prosecuted. Any man who forces a woman to have sex, including a woman's husband, can be charged with rape.

It is important for any woman in this situation to get help as soon as possible. A solicitor or the Citizens Advice Bureau can explain the available options. In some areas there are safe places for women to go and stay in called refuges or shelters. There are emergency telephone numbers in the Helpline section at the front of the Yellow Pages including, for women, the number of the nearest Women's Centre. The police can also help women find a safe place to stay.

## Parents' responsibilities

The law says that parents of a child who are married to one another have equal responsibility for their child. This continues even if the parents separate or divorce. But when a child's parents are not married, only the mother has parental responsibility unless:

- the father jointly registers the child's birth with the mother

- the father subsequently marries the mother

- the father obtains the mother's agreement for equal parental responsibility

- the father acquires parental responsibility by applying to court.

Parental responsibility continues until a child is 18 years old.

## Support

Both parents, whether they are married to each other or not, have a legal responsibility to maintain their children financially. A father who does not have parental responsibility in law still has a duty to support his children financially.

## Control

Parents are responsible for the care and control of their children until they are 18. By law, they can use reasonable force to discipline them, but if this punishment is too severe, they can be prosecuted for assault or the child may be taken into the care of the local authority.

Many voluntary organisations and local authorities offer parenting courses, support and advice on being a parent. Parentline Plus is a national charity that works for, and with, parents. They offer a free 24-hour, 7 days a week telephone: helpline service for parents-telephone: 0808 800 202, or: www.parentlineplus.org.uk You can also get information on parenting on the BBC website: www.bbc.co.uk/parenting

## Child protection

Every local authority has a legal duty to protect all children in its area from danger, and must place the safety and interest of the child above all else. If it believes that a child is suffering significant harm at home, it must take action to try and stop this happening. Where possible, local authorities try to work with parents, but they have the power to take a child from its home and into care. This is only done in an emergency or when all other possibilities have failed.

ChildLine is a free and confidential helpline for children and young people in the UK to talk about any problem with a counsellor - telephone: 0800 1111, or: www.childline.org.uk In the UK, there are laws about employment and children (see chapter 6).

## Medical advice and treatment for children and young people

From the age of 16, young people do not need their parents' permission for medical consultation or treatment as long as the doctor or nurse believes that the young person fully understands what is involved. If a young person under the age of 16 asks for contraceptive advice and treatment, the doctor will encourage them to discuss this with a parent or carer. But most doctors will prescribe contraception for a young person if they believe they are able to understand what is involved.

## Leaving a child on their own

As a general rule, it is against the law for children to be left alone in the home unless they are in the care of a responsible person aged 16 or over.

# Consumer protection

Childminders and nurseries must be registered and inspected by the Office for Standards in Education (Ofsted). You can get details of registered childminders in your area from your local authority Children's Information Service (CIS). ChildcareLink on 08000 96 02 96 or www.childcarelink.gov.uk can give you the telephone number of your local CIS. You can also contact the National Childminding Association (NCMA) on 0800 169 4486 or www.ncma.org.uk

By law, when you buy something from a shop, it should do everything you can reasonably expect and all that the seller and manufacturer claim. The Sale of Goods Act 1979 states that the goods you buy from a shop or trader must:

- be of satisfactory quality, and

- match the description, and

- be fit for all their intended purposes.

## Satisfactory quality

'Being of satisfactory quality' means the goods must be free from faults, scratches or damage - unless the sales assistant told you about the fault or you had a chance to look carefully at the item before you bought it and had the opportunity to find the fault.

This rule applies to any goods you buy from a shop or trader - new or second-hand. But it does not apply to goods bought privately from an individual, for example through a newspaper or shop window advertisement. In these cases, the buyer is expected to take responsibility for the quality of the goods they buy.

**Check that you understand:**

- What the Human Rights Act is

- What equal opportunities means and how to get more information about it

- The laws about marriage, divorce and domestic violence

- The laws about parental responsibility for children

- How to get support about parenting

- Children's rights and support for children and young people

## Match the description

'Matching the description' means that the goods you buy must be the same as the description on the packaging or advertisement at the time of sale. This rule applies to all goods sold, including second-hand goods sold privately.

## Fit for all their intended purposes

'Being fit for all their intended purposes' means that the goods must do what the seller, packaging or advertiser claims.

## Taking care with your purchases

Sometimes there are problems with goods bought from shops, by mail order or on the internet and so it is a good idea to take the following steps:

- be cautious of advertisements that make exaggerated claims, and of people who try to sell you things at your door

- keep receipts as proof of purchase, particularly if the goods were expensive

- if there is a problem with something you bought, stop using it straight away and tell the shop or trader about the problem

- if you have to make a complaint to a shop or company, keep a record of telephone calls and make a copy of any letters or emails that you send.

Prices are usually clearly marked on most new goods and these are the prices that customers expect to pay. In general, people in the UK do not barter or negotiate prices for goods. But some bargaining may take place when buying houses, second-hand goods such as cars, or some household services such as decorating or gardening.

## Services

The law covering services - such as hairdressing or shoe repairs - states that services must be done:

- with reasonable care and skill

- within a reasonable time

- for a reasonable charge.

To avoid problems it is a good idea to agree the price before the work starts.

## Mail order and internet shopping

There are special regulations to protect people who buy goods from home, by post, phone or on the internet. As well as the rights listed above, you are entitled to cancel your order within 7 working days if you decide that you do not want to buy the item. But this does not apply to all purchases. For example, you cannot change your mind for tickets or accommodation bookings, audio and video recordings that have been opened, newspapers and magazines, and perishable items such as flowers or food. You are also entitled to a full refund if you do not receive the goods by the date agreed or within 30 days, if you did not agree a date.

If you are buying goods on the internet, it is important to make sure that you have the trader's full address. You also need to make sure that the website offers a secure way of paying - this is shown by a small picture of a yellow padlock at the bottom of the screen.

## Complaints

If a fault appears soon after you have bought an item and you are not responsible, you are entitled either to your money back or to a replacement. It is the shop's responsibility to deal with the problem.

If an item worked well at first and then developed a fault, you may still be entitled to all or some of your money back, to be offered a replacement or to have the item repaired free of charge. The action taken will depend on how long you have had the goods, how serious the fault is and whether it is unreasonable for a fault to develop so soon.

## Paying by credit card

If you have used a credit card to buy something which cost between £100 and £30,000 and there is a problem with it, you can claim the money back from the credit card company. This can be useful if the trader does not help to solve the problem or has gone out of business.

## Help and advice

You can get advice locally from the Trading Standards Office, listed in the phone book under the local authority, or from the Citizens Advice Bureau.

You can check the prices and performance of many products in *Which?*, an independent magazine. You can subscribe to the magazine or read it in the reference department of most public libraries.

There is more information about consumer rights from the BBC website: www.bbc.co.uk You can also get information from the government's official department which protects consumers - the Office of Fair Trading, www.oft.gov.uk

**Check that you understand:**

- Consumer rights for items bought in shops and by mail order, phone or on the internet

- Consumer rights for services

- How to make complaints and get help and advice

# Chapter 8

# SOURCES OF HELP AND INFORMATION

## Introduction

In this chapter there is information about:

- Help for refugees and asylum seekers

- Libraries

- The Citizens Advice Bureau

- The police

- Sources of information

- The internet

and general tips on how to get information and advice

In the UK, there are many different organisations offering all kinds of help and advice. In other chapters of this book there are details of where to go to get further information on a particular subject. This section tells you more about the services offered by advice centres, libraries and about other sources of information.

### Be prepared

When you are looking for information or help, consider the following advice:

- Before you ask for information think carefully about what you need to know. Make a few notes about the key things you want to know

- Take a pen and paper to make notes about the information you receive

- If you do not understand English very well, take someone with you to help, or ask if there is an interpreter available

# Public libraries

- Take all the relevant documents with you. Sometimes you will have an account or reference number for your case

- Try to avoid long explanations

- Make a note of the name of the person you talk to so you can refer to it if you need to phone or visit again.

Every town and city in the UK has one or more public libraries. You can find the address of your local library in the phone book. Most of the services offered by public libraries are free. They are paid for by national and local taxes. Anyone may use a local library, but if you want to borrow books and other items you usually have to become a member. To become a member you usually have to show proof of your identity and your address.

## Children

There is usually a separate section of the library for children. Libraries encourage children to read books and sometimes there are special reading activities for children.

## Books and other items

Members can borrow books for a specific period of time. At some libraries it is possible to borrow CDs, audiotapes and DVDs. There are often books in languages other than English. There are also books on audiotape (called 'talking books') and books with large print for people with sight problems. If you do not return books and other items on time, you will have to pay a fine. If the library does not have a book you need, they can usually order it for you from another library.

## Reference

In the reference section there are books such as dictionaries, encyclopaedias, telephone directories, Yellow Pages and Thomson Local guides. Sometimes there are newspapers. The reference section is helpful if you need information on something in particular. The library is also a good place to ask about local and community facilities and events. If you do not understand English very well, some libraries might offer a translation service.

## Computers, photocopiers and fax machines

Libraries also have computers which the public can use to do word processing, send and receive emails and browse the internet. It is also possible in some libraries to photocopy and to send faxes. There might be a charge for these services.

## Citizens Advice Bureau

The Citizens Advice Bureau (CAB) gives free, confidential and impartial advice. It is an independent organisation with trained advisers. Most towns and cities have a CAB office. You can find the address in the phone book, the local library or visit the CAB website at www.nacab.org.uk. Before you visit a CAB office you should check the opening times of your local office. Help is also available by email. Details about this are available on the website.

### Practical help

CABs give advice and help across a wide range of topics. These include money, benefits, pensions, employment, the NHS, housing, immigration, domestic violence and consumer problems.

The CAB can also help with completing forms and writing letters. They can also help if you have to go to court or a tribunal. If you have problems understanding English they may be able to provide interpreters. The CAB also runs an information website at www.adviceguide.org.uk which gives information on a wide range of topics. It is available in English, Welsh, Bengali, Chinese, Gujarati, Punjabi and Urdu.

## The police service

The main role of the police is to deal with crime, but they also offer protection and assistance to the public. They are expected to be friendly and helpful to people seeking their assistance. If you are worried about your personal safety or have a question about the law or crime, the police will be able to help you. In some parts of the country there are special telephone information lines for this purpose. In many communities there are community support officers (CSOs) who work at a local level to provide a visible presence on the streets and reassure local people. They may give talks on safety issues in schools and community centres and generally help the police with their local duties.

### Contacting the police

If you need advice or you need to report a crime which is not dangerous or life-threatening you should phone the local police station. The number is in the telephone book under 'Police'. DO NOT phone 999 or 112 unless there is an emergency.

If there is a danger to life or a crime in progress, dial 999 or 112. The operator will ask which service you require: police, fire, ambulance or coastguard service. You will be asked where you are calling from and the location of the accident or emergency. Do not call 999 or 112 under any other circumstances.

## The Fire Service

The fire service (known in some areas as the fire and rescue service) can often help with fire safety and fire prevention. This includes giving advice about what to do if there is a fire, how to make a fire escape plan for you and your family and advice on fire hazards in the home. In some areas there are free home fire safety checks and the fire service might also be able to fit smoke detectors, especially for the elderly. For further information contact your local fire service (the number is in the telephone book under 'Fire') or go to www.fire.gov.uk

- Yellow Pages: a yellow telephone directory which gives details of organisations, services and businesses in the local area. There is also a website at: www.yell.com

- Thomson Local: a guide to your local area (available in Great Britain), similar to the Yellow Pages.

- Local authorities: all give information about their services such as education and social services. The numbers for each section of the local authority can be found in the phone book. Most local authorities have useful websites. Some have information and advice centres open to the public.

- Tourist information centres: give information about local attractions as well as on transport, places of worship, doctor's surgeries and so on.

- Post offices: the main role of the post office is to collect and deliver mail. They also provide information about benefits and state pensions. You can also open a bank account at the post office and pay bills. At the post office you get application forms for driving licences, other licences and passports. They can also check passport applications before you send them to the passport office.

- Helplines: many organisations have special telephone lines which give advice on specific issues or problems. You can get these from the CAB or public library or from the internet (see below).

- Newspapers: these are either national or local. Local newspapers are good for local information such as the opening times of late-night chemists.

- Television and radio channels: these are either national or local. Local radio stations can be a good source of local information.

- Directgov: this is a government-sponsored website that gives information about local and national government issues, ranging from how you complete a tax return to how you renew a library book, www.direct.gov.uk

## Using the internet

The internet can be accessed through a computer either at home, in the local library or in an internet café. To get information from the internet you need to know the address of a specific website (this usually begins with 'www') or you need to use a search engine. The most popular search engine is Google at: www.google.co.uk

The search engine uses key words to find information about a specific thing. If you enter the key words (consumer rights, for example) into the search engine, it will look for both words separately and give you millions of results. If you put inverted commas around the words ('consumer rights') the search engine will look for websites only with words in this combination.

## Websites

There are many addresses of useful websites in this guide. A particularly useful website is the BBC website at: www.bbc.co.uk This gives you access to local, national and international information and has a news service in over 40 languages. It also has sections on education, history, science, business and law and provides links to other valuable sources of information.

## Make sure you understand:

- What services libraries offer

- What services Citizens Advice Bureaux offer

- What help and advice you can get from the police

- When you should phone 999 or 112, and when you should NOT phone those numbers

- There are many sources of advice and information in the UK, such as the local authority, the post office and advice centres

- There are also helplines and other resources, such as local newspapers and telephone directories

- The internet is a very useful source of information

# Chapter 9: BUILDING BETTER COMMUNITIES

## Cohesive communities

Becoming a British Citizen or becoming settled in the UK brings opportunities but also responsibilities. This section looks at some of the responsibilities and gives information about some of the many ways in which people can help to make their communities a better place to live and work.

Although Britain is one of the world's most diverse societies, most people believe that there should be a set of shared values with which everyone can agree. Many of those values are mentioned in other parts of this book. There is a general principle that all people should respect the law and the rights of others. But in addition to obeying the law, people want to get on well with their neighbours and contribute to the well-being of all. The purpose of this book is to help new migrants who want to become settled in the UK or to become British Citizens to become more aware of the laws, customs and traditions here. Knowing about these things will make it easier to become a full and active citizen, but reading a book is no substitute for being part of society. By getting to know and understand your community, life will be better for everyone.

Surveys have given us some very interesting information about what makes people feel good or bad about the area they live in. Everyone should try to be a good neighbour. You can start to do this by introducing yourself to the people who live next to you. It is good to avoid making too much noise and to respect the privacy of your neighbours. One of the most common causes of complaint about neighbours is about leaving rubbish outside the house. So make sure you know what days you can put out your rubbish for it to be collected and that you know what arrangements there are in your area for recycling.

## Good citizens

A special survey - the UK Citizenship Survey in 2005 - told us a great deal about what people think about the rights and responsibilities of being a citizen. The things that people strongly felt should be the responsibilities of all people living in the UK were:

- to obey and respect the law
- to raise children properly
- to treat others with fairness and respect
- to behave responsibly
- to help and protect your family
- to respect and preserve the environment
- to behave morally and ethically
- to treat all races equally
- to work to provide for yourself
- to help others
- to vote.

## Supporting the community

There are a number of positive ways in which you can be a good citizen. These include:

## Jury service

Apart from getting the right to vote, people on the electoral register might be asked to serve on a jury (see page 119). Jurors are chosen at random from the electoral register. Anyone who is on the electoral register and is aged 18-70 can be asked to serve. The task of jurors is to decide the outcome of a criminal trial in the Crown Court. They will be among many people chosen each year for jury service and they will have an opportunity to be involved in the legal system. Jurors hear the more serious criminal cases such as theft, burglary, and drugs offences. Jurors also hear cases involving murder and rape, although these types of cases are less common.

Their task is to consider the evidence presented throughout the trial and then reach a verdict of 'guilty' or 'not guilty' based on that evidence.

Because jurors are randomly selected they represent all sections of society. They will be asked to take an unbiased approach to the case to ensure that a fair trial takes place. Being a juror is a very important role and is a chance to do something positive for the community. Some people are not qualified for jury service and others might be excused from doing it. More details can be found on the Department for Constitutional Affairs website, www.dca.gov.uk

Helping at schools

If you have children, there are many ways in which you can help at their schools. Often, parents can help in classrooms or during mealtimes by helping to supervise activities or helping children with their reading. Often you will find out about these opportunities by notices in the school or from notes your children bring home.

Many schools organise events to raise money for extra equipment or out of school activities. Activities might include book sales, toy sales, or bringing food to sell. You might have good ideas of your own for raising money. Sometimes events are organised by parent and staff associations (PSAs). These are also known as parent teacher associations (PTAs) and volunteering to help with events or joining the association is a way of doing something good for the school and also making new friends in your local community.

School governors

School governors are people from the school community who wish to make a positive contribution to children's education. They must be aged 18 or over at the date of their election or appointment. There is no upper age limit.

Governors are a large volunteer force and have an important part to play in raising school standards. They have three key roles of setting strategic direction, ensuring accountability and monitoring and evaluating school performance.

You can contact your local school to ask if they need a new governor. Your local education authority (LEA) will be able to help you find a school or advise on opportunities to become an LEA governor.

Political parties

Political parties always welcome new members, and joining a political party is an important way of demonstrating support for the views you hold and for the democratic process. Political parties are especially busy at election times, when their members work hard to persuade people to vote for their candidates, for instance by handing out leaflets in the street or by knocking on people's doors and asking for their support. Becoming a British citizen allows you to stand for office as a local councillor or as a Member of Parliament and so provides an opportunity for becoming even more involved in the political life of the UK.

## Local services

Many local service providers want to involve local people in decisions about the way in which they work. There are opportunities to serve as a Board member in Primary Care Trusts or Regional Development Agencies. Universities, local Learning and Skills Councils, housing associations and arts councils also advertise for people to serve as volunteers in their governing bodies. It is also possible to become a lay (non-police) representative on a police authority or even to apply to become a magistrate. You will often find advertisements for vacancies in your local newspaper or on local radio.

## Volunteering

Volunteering is working for good causes without payment. There are many benefits from volunteering. It gives you a chance to meet new people and can help if you are bored at home. Some volunteer activities might help you by giving you a chance to practise your English or to give you work skills that will help you find a job or improve your CV. But many people volunteer simply because they want to do something to help other people.

Activities you can do as a volunteer include:

- helping the elderly
- youth work
- helping improve the environment
- working with the homeless
- mentoring
- work in health and hospitals
- working with animals.

Many charities want volunteers to help with their activities and to help them raise money. They often advertise in local newspapers and most charities have websites that will give you more information. If you want to volunteer you can get more information from www.do-it.org.uk which is a database of thousands of volunteering opportunities.

In recognition of the important role volunteers and the not-for-profit sector play in both society and the economy, the Office of the Third Sector (OTS) was set up in May 2006 to drive forward the Government's role in supporting a thriving voluntary sector. The third sector includes voluntary and community organisations, charities, social enterprises and faith groups.

The OTS brings together the work of the former Active Communities Directorate (ACD), originally in the Home Office and the Social Enterprise Unit (SEnU), formerly in the Department of Trade and Industry (DTI) within the Cabinet Office. It will work closely with the Department for Communities and Local Government (DCLG) on the role of third-sector organisations in communities and decision-making at a local and regional level. For more information, visit the Office of the Third Sector website at: www.cabinetoffice.gov.uk/thirdsector

For younger people, Millenium Volunteers (MV) is a national programme aimed at people aged 16-24. As an MV you get a chance to help others by doing something you enjoy and develop your skills at the same time. There are schemes in most cities and towns. If you do 200 hours of volunteering, you get an Award of Excellence. For more information go to www.milleniumvolunteers.gov.uk

TimeBank is a national charity that seeks to inspire and connect people to share and give their time. TimeBank appeals to people who know that their time and skills are in demand - but just don't know what to do about it or where to start. TimeBank has worked in partnership with Government departments in finding volunteers to help with disadvantaged people. For example, TimeBank has worked with the Home Office to find volunteers to work with refugees as their mentors-to help them find jobs and to get more involved in society. For more information go to www.timebank.org.uk

Community Service Volunteers (CSV) is one of the largest organisations in the UK that promotes volunteering. It prides itself on pioneering new solutions and innovative ways to tackle society's needs and has over 40 years' experience in supporting partners and volunteers in activities that really make a difference to people's lives.

CSV's campaign to promote volunteering, CSV Make a Difference Day, is the UK's biggest day of direct volunteering in the community. CSV has over 10,000 senior volunteers who run activities and projects for CSV and recruit other senior volunteers. For more information go to www.csv.org.uk

The Prince's Trust was founded in 1976 by The Prince of Wales. Having completed his duty in the Royal Navy, he became dedicated to improving the lives of disadvantaged young people in the UK, and began the Trust to deliver on that commitment.

The Trust has become the UK's leading youth charity, offering a range of opportunities including training, personal development, support in starting up a business, mentoring and advice for young people aged 14-30.

The Trust has four key target groups:

- unemployed young people
- young people underachieving
- young people leaving care
- young offenders and ex-offenders.

All of these activities need volunteers. Many new or aspiring managers find that volunteering with a Prince's Trust group helps them with their own career as they have to tackle real management issues in a challenging environment. If you want to volunteer to help disadvantaged young people you can contact the Trust at www.princes-trust.org.uk

Charities

Britain has many thousands of active charities, working to improve the lives of people - and animals - in a wide variety of ways. Some of the organisations already mentioned in this chapter are charities, but you will hear about the work of many others. A few of the most important charities working in Britain are described below.

## Comic Relief

Red Nose Day is a fund-raising event that takes place every two years. Comic Relief, the organisation behind it, was set up by comedians and uses comedy and laughter to get serious messages across, while making sure that everyone who gets involved can have fun at the same time. Its objective is to raise money for deserving causes. Everything raised is distributed to well-known charities and is used for good work both in the UK and abroad.

Red Nose Day culminates in a night of comedy and moving documentary films on television. Everyone in England, Scotland, Wales and Northern Ireland is encouraged to cast inhibitions aside, put on a Red Nose and do something a bit silly to raise money. It is an event that unites people in trying to make a difference to the lives of thousands of individuals facing terrible injustice or living in extreme poverty. The website for more information is www.comicrelief.com

## British Red Cross

The British Red Cross is a member of the International Red Cross and Red Crescent movement, the world's largest humanitarian organisation. The movement champions individual and community values which encourage respect for other human beings and a willingness to work together to find solutions to community problems. The Red Cross/Red Crescent movement is committed to, and bound by, its Fundamental Principles.

These are:

- Humanity
- Impartiality
- Neutrality
- Independence
- Voluntary service
- Unity
- Universality.

It has no religious affiliation and in the UK offers volunteering opportunities in many fields, including first aid, emergency response, a message and tracing service to try to reunite people who have been separated by conflict, and helping refugees.

## Friends of the Earth

Friends of the Earth is one of the leading environmental charities in the UK and was founded in 1971. Further information can be obtained from its website at www.foe.org.uk Its interests are:

- Getting a grip on climate change
- Bringing in laws to bring recycling to your doorstep.
- Warmer, more energy efficient homes
- Protecting our countryside.
- Keeping genetically modified food off the menu.
- Persuading big companies to behave better in respect of the environment.

## Greenpeace

## Worldwide Fund for Nature

Greenpeace (www. greenpeace.org.uk) is an international environmental organisation founded in Vancouver, British Columbia, Canada in 1971. It is known for its campaigns to stop atmospheric and underground nuclear testing as well as to bring an end to high-seas whaling. In later years, the focus of the organisation turned to other environmental issues, including bottom trawling, global warming, ancient forest destruction, nuclear power and genetic engineering. Greenpeace has national and regional offices in 41 countries worldwide, including the UK. It receives its income through the individual contributions of an estimated 2.8 million financial supporters, as well as from grants from charitable foundations, but does not accept funding from governments or corporations.

Greenpeace's official mission statement describes the organisation and its aims thus:

Greenpeace is an independent, campaigning organisation which uses non-violent, creative confrontation to expose global environmental problems, and to force solutions for a green and peaceful future. Greenpeace's goal is to ensure the ability of the earth to nurture life in all its diversity.

This charity used to be known as the World Wildlife Fund and was founded in 1961. WWF-UK works on both global and local environmental issues. Much of its work is in areas where the most critically endangered wildlife and the least protected habitats are found. It believes, however, that the origins of many environmental problems lie in developed countries, including, for example, our consumption of natural resources.

WWF-UK not only directs some 70 per cent of its conservation expenditure towards its global programmes but also seeks to influence global environmental issues through responsible actions in the UK. Its website is at www.wwf.org.uk

## Oxfam

This well-known charity has its origins during the Second World War, when Greece was occupied by the Nazis and suffered a serious famine. The Oxford Committee for Famine Relief was set up in 1942 in order to raise money and persuade the British government to intervene to help the victims of famine. After the war the Oxford Committee saw a continuing need and enlarged its objectives to include 'the relief of suffering in consequence of the war'. Activity then centred on the provision of food parcels

and clothing to Europe. Today, Oxfam responds in emergencies to save lives; works with people to improve their lives and prospects through longer term development programmes; and campaigns on issues that they believe will achieve lasting change and an end to poverty. Its website is at www.oxfam.org.uk

There are many other charities and voluntary organisations that would appreciate you giving up some of your time or your skills. They all have different aims but they all have something in common - the wish to help others and to make our lives and our communities better.

**gloss** unfavourable) comments *on.* [alt. of GLOZE a[...]
L *glossa*]

**glŏss²** *n.,* & *v.t.* **1.** *n.* superficial lustre;[...]
external appearance; ~ **paint** etc.[...]
varnish to give glossy finish). **2.** *v.t.* ma[...]
(**over**), give specious appearance to, see[...]
[16th c., of unkn. orig.]

**glŏ′ssal** *a.* (Anat.) of the tongue, lingu[...]
tongue + -AL]

**glŏ′ssar|y̆** *n.* collection of glosses; list [...]
of abstruse, obsolete, dialectal, or[...]
partial dictionary; hence **glŏssar̄**[...]
[f. L *glossarium* (*glossa* GLOSS¹; see [...]

**glŏssā′tor** *n.* writer of glosses, c[...]
medieval law-texts. [ME f. me[...]
GLOSS¹; see -OR)]

**glŏ′ssēme** *n.* feature of a[...]
meaning and does not consi[...]
units. [f. Gk *glōssēma* (*glōssa* [...]

**glŏssī′tis** *n.* inflammation [...]
tongue + -ITIS]

**glŏssō-** *comb. form.* **1.** to[...]
tongue and larynx. **2.** = [...]
*n.,* commentator, g[...]
[...]a l f. Gk *glōssa* [...]
[...]′lia *n.* gift of [...]

# GLOSSARY

This glossary will help readers to understand the meanings of key words and key expressions in the ways in which they are used and the contexts in which they appear in this handbook.

Some words or expressions in the definitions are written in bold. This can mean any of the following:

- they are explained in another part of the glossary

- they share the same kind of meaning as a word that is being defined but are used in another way in a sentence

- they relate to the word that is being defined in some way, e.g. they have an exact opposite meaning or a very similar one - in this case, the word/s will be bracketed and preceded by 'see', e.g. (see vocational courses).

When words may be difficult to understand, an example of use may follow the definition.

The word that is bracketed after an entry relates to the particular context in which the word is being defined, e.g. applicant (employment).

A slash/separates different definitions.

The convention s/he is used to mean 'she or he'.

| | |
|---|---|
| absent from work | not at work, e.g. because of illness |
| abusive | unkind or violent - usually used to describe behaviour towards another person |
| academic course | a series of lessons in which a student learns by studying information that s/he reads in books (see vocational course) |
| access (internet) | connect to/connection |
| accountant | a person whose job is to keep business records, to work out how much money a person or business is making or losing, and how much business tax needs to be paid (see business accounts) |
| AD | Anno Domini - referring to the number of years after Christ was born - used as a time reference, e.g. the Romans left Britain in 410 AD (see BC) |
| addictive substance | usually a type of drug that a person feels a strong need to take very often, and finds very difficult to stop using |
| adultery | sex between a married person and someone who is not their husband or wife |
| afford | have enough money to pay for something |
| allegiance | loyalty to something, e.g. to a leader, a faith, a country or a cultural tradition |
| amphetamine | a type of drug which is addictive, powerful and illegal (see addictive substances) |
| annexation | taking control of a neighbouring country, usually by force |

| | |
|---|---|
| **anonymous information** | information which is given by someone whose name is unknown |
| **ante-natal care** | medical care given to a woman (and to her unborn baby) while she is pregnant |
| **applicant (employment)** | someone who has asked an employer to give them a particular job - people often apply for jobs by writing a letter or completing a form |
| **application letter** | a formal letter sent to an employer asking for (applying for) a job |
| **appoint (employment)** | choose someone to do a job and formally offer it to them |
| **arbitrary (law)** | not bound by rules or law, and sometimes thought to be unfair |
| **aristocracy** | a group of people who are born into the highest class in society and who are traditionally very rich - a member of the aristocracy is called an aristocrat |
| **armed forces** | the army, navy and air force which defend a country in times of peace and war |
| **arrested (police)** | taken by the police to a police station and made to stay there to answer questions about illegal actions or activity (see detained by the police) |
| **assault** | the criminal act of using physical force against someone or of attacking someone, e.g. hitting someone |
| **assessment methods (education)** | ways to measure a student's abilities or skills, e.g. a teacher can assess a child's reading and writing skills using a variety of different methods |
| **asylum** | a place where people, who are accused of crime in another country, can live in safety |

**asylum seekers**   people who leave their own country because they feel it is too dangerous for them to stay there (usually because of political reasons) and who then formally ask to stay in another country where it will be safer for them to live (see refugees)

---

**ban**   officially forbid

**Bank Holiday**   a day when most people have an official day off work and when banks and most other businesses are closed-a Bank Holiday can also be called a public holiday

**baron**   a man who is a member of the lower ranks of British nobility

**BC**   Before Christ-referring to the number of years before Christ was born-used as a time reference, e.g. 750 BC (see AD)

**betting shop**   a place where a person can go and pay to try to win money by gambling on the results of horse racing, football matches etc.

**bid (money)**   offer to pay a price for something when the cost is not fixed - other interested buyers may join in the bidding and the item will be sold to the highest bidder (the person who makes the highest offer)

**binding, legally**   an agreement to do something which, by law, cannot be changed or be withdrawn from

**birth certificate**   an official document that states the name of a person, the place and date of his/her birth, and the names and occupations of his/her parents

**birth parent**   a mother or father who is the natural, biological parent of a child

**birth rate**   the number of babies born, expressed as a percentage of a population, in a particular year or place

**bishop**   a senior priest in a Christian religion who is the head of different churches in a specified area

**boom**   a sharp rise in something - very often in business activity

**bound, legally**   obliged to do something in a way that follows certain laws

**breach of contract**   a situation arising when a person breaks a legal agreement to do or not to do something

**British Empire**   a large number of states under British colonial rule and which, at one time in history, accounted for one-quarter of the world's population. Many of these states are now independent; the rest are collectively known as the Commonwealth of Nations

**broker (finance)**   a person whose job is to give advice and to help select the most suitable and best-value service in areas such as insurance and mortgages, also called a financial adviser

**brutality**   behaviour towards another person that is cruel and violent and causes harm

**building society**   a kind of bank which can be used for saving money or for borrowing money from in order to buy a house (see mortgage)

**built-up area**   a place where there are a lot of buildings and not many open spaces and where a lot of people live and/or work

**bureaux de change**   places where people can exchange one currency for another, e.g. they can sell pounds to buy euros

**burglary**    the criminal act of entering and stealing something from a building (see theft)

**bursary**    money in the form of a grant that a university gives to a student so they can study at university

**business accounts**    an official record of the amount of money a business is making, and how much it is paying for services or equipment etc, that is used to calculate the amount of tax that must be paid to the government (see accountant)

**by-election**    election which is held when an MP resigns or dies and when a new MP needs to be elected to replace him/her in Parliament before the next general election

---

**Cabinet (government)**    a group of senior ministers who are responsible for controlling government policy

**cable company**    a company that can supply customers with a telephone or cable television connection

**cannabis**    an illegal drug that is usually smoked

**captivity**    being held in prison, not being allowed to move freely

**carriageway**    a single carriageway is a road which is only wide enough for one lane of traffic and which is divided from another road which takes traffic going in the opposite direction

**a dual carriageway**    is a road which is wide enough for two lanes of traffic and which is divided from another road which takes traffic in the opposite direction

**cast a vote (government)**    formally register one choice from a number of options so that a group decision can be made about the most popular outcome, e.g. so that the MP with the largest number of supporters is the one who is elected

**casualties (medical)**    people who are wounded, e.g. in an accident or in war

**caution (employment, law)**    a formal warning about something

**cautious**    careful, not wanting to get into a dangerous situation

**census (government)**    an official count of the number of people who live in a country and possibly including information about those people, e.g. age, race, marital status etc.

**charity, give to**    give money or take action to help people who are suffering from poverty, illnesses, starvation etc.

**charter (government)**    an official written statement which describes the rights and responsibilities of a state and its citizens

**chieftain**    ruler or leader of a clan in Scotland

**childminder**    a person whose job is to look after young children, usually while the children's parents are at work - a childminder usually has a qualification to do this kind of work

**circulate (money)**    pass from one person to another and then to another etc.

**civil disobedience**    the refusal of members of the public to obey laws, often because they want to protest against political issues

| | |
|---|---|
| **civil law** | the legal system that deals with disputes between people or groups of people, e.g. domestic arguments, divorce, problems between landlords and tenants |
| **civil service** | the departments within government which manage the business of running the country – people who work for the government can be called civil servants |
| **clamp (transport, police)** | a metal device that is put on the wheel of a car to prevent it from being driven away (usually used because the car is parked somewhere illegally) – the driver will have to pay to have the clamp removed |
| **clan** | a group of people or families who live under the rule of a chieftain and who are sometimes descendants of the same ancestor – this is a term traditionally used in Scotland |
| **clarification (language)** | a clear way of saying something that is easy to understand |
| **clergy** | Christian church officials, e.g. priests and bishops |
| **coalition** | a partnership between different political parties |
| **cocaine** | a type of drug which is addictive, powerful and illegal. It can be used by doctors to control pain (see addictive substances) |
| **code of practice** | an agreed set of professional rules and procedures that someone in work is expected to follow |
| **colleagues** | people who work together in the same company and who often have professional jobs |
| **colonise** | inhabit and take control of another country for the wealth and benefit of the home country – the people who move in and take control are called colonists |

| | |
|---|---|
| **commemorate** | do something to show that something or someone important is remembered, usually on a particular day |
| **commit a crime** | do something which is against the law (see criminal, criminal offence) |
| **Commonwealth of Nations** | an association of Britain and of sovereign states that used to be British colonies or states that are still ruled by Britain - the British monarch is accepted by the Commonwealth countries as their ruler |
| **community events** | events which are organised within a local area to help, in some way, the people who live or work in the same area, e.g. a town might hold a community event in order to raise money to buy special equipment for a local school |
| **compensation (money)** | money which must be paid to someone because they have suffered in some way, e.g. loss, injury. Compensation can also be paid to a person if their employer has treated them unfairly or illegally |
| **compulsory testing** | tests which must be done by law |
| **concern** | worry about an important problem/a worrying thing |
| **concession** | a right which is given to someone to end an argument or disagreement |
| **condemn to death** | a situation where a criminal is found guilty of such a serious crime that the judge decides to give the most severe punishment possible, which is death-this does not happen in the UK |
| **confidential information** | information that is private and secret and only known to the giver and receiver of that information |

**confiscate (law)**     legally take possessions or property from the person who owns them

**conquered**     beaten in battle

**consecutive**     following one another without a break or interruption, e.g. next week we must have meetings on two consecutive days, Tuesday and Wednesday

**constituency**     a specific area where the voters who live in that place (its constituents) can elect an MP to represent them in Parliament

**constitution (law)**     the legal structure of established laws and principles which is used to govern a country

**consumer problems**     problems which people have that are to do with things that they have bought or services that they have paid for

**contraception**     methods used to prevent women who have sex from becoming pregnant, e.g. taking contraceptive pills, using a condom

**contributions (finance)**     money paid regularly by someone which will help pay for something which is worth much more, e.g. a pension

**convention (government)**     an official agreement, usually between countries, about particular rules or codes of behaviour

**corrupt (behaviour)**     acting in a dishonest and illegal way

**coverage (media)**     newspaper reports that can be read in the press (see free press)

| | |
|---|---|
| **credit card** | a card which a person can use to buy goods or services which are paid for by a credit company - the credit company then sends the card-holder a monthly bill - goods can therefore be bought, but paid for later (see debit card) |
| **criminal** | a person who is found guilty of breaking the law |
| **criminal offence** | an illegal activity, e.g. burglary, for which the criminal may be prosecuted |
| **Crusades** | wars fought to try to spread Christianity |
| **currency (money)** | a particular system of money that a country or group of countries use, e.g. in the EU, the form of currency that is used most widely is the euro |
| **cut off (service)** | disconnect the supply of something |
| **debate** | a discussion in which people give different opinions about something/to discuss and give different opinions about something |
| **debit card** | a card which a person can use to buy goods or services with money that is in their bank or building society account - the money is taken from their account automatically (see credit card) |
| **decline in number** | reduce, decrease, fall, go down |
| **decree (law)** | official order, law or decision |
| **defeat** | to be stronger than an opponent and therefore win a battle, a war, a competition etc. |
| **defer** | delay until a later time |

**degrading (treatment)**  treatment that causes humiliation (see humiliated)

**democratic country**  a country which is governed by people who are elected by the population to represent them in Parliament

**deport**  make someone leave a country and, usually, return to the country from which they originally came - this is because the person who must be deported does not have the legal right to stay

**deposit (housing)**  an amount of money paid to a landlord when a person rents a flat or house - this money is given back when the person leaves, but only if the property or furniture has not been damaged

**deposit (money)**  an amount of money that is only part of the full price of something - the rest, 'the balance', must be paid later

**descent, of**  coming originally from, e.g. of Indian descent means being a member of a family coming originally from India (see roots, ethnic origin)

**desert someone (law)**  leave someone and not come back to help or look after them, e.g. to leave a husband or wife

**detained by the police**  kept at a police station and not allowed to leave (see arrested)

**detect crimes (police)**  discover and find out information about illegal actions or activities

**devolution**  the passing of power from a central government to another group at a regional or local level which can then be called a devolved administration

**dialect**  a form of a language which is spoken only by a particular social group or by a group of people living in a particular area

**direct debit**  an arrangement that a person makes to transfer an amount of money from his/her bank account into another account on a regular basis (see standing order)

**disability, physical/ mental**  a condition that a person has that makes doing ordinary things like walking, seeing, speaking, talking, or learning difficult

**discrimination**  the act of treating an individual or a particular group of people in a way which is unfair, for example because of their race, nationality, sex, sexuality, age, or disability. Paying a woman less than a man for the same work is an example of discrimination

**dismissal (employment)**  removal from a job, the 'sack'

**disputes**  arguments or disagreements that are serious and about which people may take legal advice or action

**disturbance (law)**  a situation where people act in a loud or violent way and which upsets or disturbs other people, e.g. fighting in a public place

**divorce**  the legal end of a marriage/the act of ending a marriage

**domestic policies**  political decisions that relate to what is happening within a country (as opposed to in another country)

**domestic rates**  a type of tax in Northern Ireland which is paid by residents to their local authority and which helps to pay for local services, e.g. education, road repairs, policing, refuse collection

**domestic violence**     fighting or acting aggressively in the home and causing mental or physical harm to someone in the family

**dominion**     a country which was once colonised but that is now self-governing

**dump**     get rid of something, throw away-often in a place where rubbish should not be left/a place where rubbish is left in an untidy and unhealthy way

**dwelling**     a place where people live, e.g. a house, a flat

**dynasty**     a situation in which power is transferred from one member of a family to another and another over a long period of time, e.g. a son becomes king after his father before him and his grandfather before that

---

**ecstasy**     a type of drug which is illegal and dangerous. It makes users feel that they have lots of energy but can cause death (see addictive substances)

**elect a person**     choose someone by voting for them

**electoral register**     the official list of all the people in a country who are allowed to vote in an election

**electorate**     all the people who are allowed to vote in an election

**eligible**     allowed by law

**emergency services**     services that can be telephoned and that will come to the help of people when they need it quickly and very urgently, e.g. the police service, the fire service, the ambulance service, the coastguard service and, at sea, the lifeguard service

| | |
|---|---|
| **employ** | give someone work and pay them to do it |
| **employee** | someone who is paid by an employer to do a job |
| **employer** | a person or company that gives work to other people and pays them for doing it |
| **engagement (family)** | an agreement between two people that they will get married at some time in the future – these people are engaged to one another but not married yet (see fiancé and fiancée) |
| **enterprise (business)** | business energy – the starting and running of business activities |
| **entitled (law)** | officially allowed (to do something) |
| **entrepreneurial** | prepared to take risks with money in order to start a business/prepared to take risks with money to make more money in business |
| **ethnic minority** | a group of people who are of a different race from the race of the majority of the population in a particular country |
| **ethnic origin** | the country of birth, someone's race or the nationality of someone when they were born/ the customs and place from which a person and their family originated (see roots) |
| **European Union (or EU)** | a political and economic association of European countries which encourages trade and co-operation between its member states |
| **evict (housing)** | order someone legally to leave the house where they are living |
| **evidence, collecting** | looking for and getting information, documents or items that show for certain that something has happened, e.g. the police went to the criminal's house to collect as much evidence as possible (see proof) |

| | |
|---|---|
| **exchange rate** | the amount of money in one currency that you need to buy a certain amount of money in another currency, e.g. £1 = $1.9 (see bureaux de change). The exchange rate can vary from day to day |
| **executed** | killed as an act of punishment |
| **exiled** | sent to another country and not allowed to return as an act of political punishment |
| **expel** | force someone officially to leave an organisation of some kind |
| **exploitation** | a situation in which someone is made to do something unfairly because they are given nothing or very little for doing it, e.g. the women were exploited by their employer who paid them less than the minimum wage and also forced them to work overtime |
| **expression, freedom of** | talking about personal ideas or beliefs without getting into any legal trouble for doing so |

| | |
|---|---|
| **facilities in the community** | local services that the public can use, e.g. libraries, schools, hospitals |
| **false statement (police)** | a report that contains untruthful information, e.g. lies told in answer to police questions |
| **famine** | a situation in which there is very little food for a long time and people often die because of this |
| **fiancé** | a man who has formally agreed to marry a woman |
| **fiancée** | a woman who has formally agreed to marry a man (see engagement) |

**fine (law)** an amount of money that a person must pay because they have broken the law (see on-the-spot fines, penalty)

**firearm** any kind of gun

**first past the post** a system of election in which the candidate with the largest number of votes in a particular constituency wins a seat in Parliament

**flooding (housing)** water coming inside a property (and which probably causes damage to it)

**forced labour** work which is usually physical and which workers have to do, but do not want to do

**free press** newspapers and other reporting media that are not controlled by government and can therefore write freely, without restriction, about anything they think their readers will be interested in

**gambling (money)** risking money to try to win more money, e.g. in card games or by trying to guess the winner of a horse race or football match

**gap year (education)** a year between leaving school and going to university during which many students choose to gain experience through travelling, or to earn money by taking a job

**general election** a situation in which all the citizens of a country who are allowed to vote choose the people they wish to represent them in their government - in Britain this usually happens every five years (see MP)

**government policies** official ideas and beliefs that are agreed by a political party about how to govern the country (see party politics)

| | |
|---|---|
| **grant (money)** | an amount of money paid by an authority to help a person or organisation pay for a particular thing, e.g. an education course, a business expansion |
| **guerrilla war** | a war in which several small groups of people fight against an opposition |
| **guidance (law)** | advice about how or where to get help |
| **guilty (law)** | found by a court to have committed a crime (see innocent) |
| **hard drugs** | drugs which are illegal and are very powerful and addictive |
| **harassment (behaviour)** | rude, offensive, threatening or bullying behaviour - a word often used to describe this kind of behaviour in a workplace |
| **health authority, local** | an organisation which manages health care and from which people can get advice about where to find medical help |
| **health hazards** | things that might be dangerous to someone's health, e.g. smoking is a hazard to health because it can cause lung cancer |
| **hearing, in court** | a meeting in court when a judge hears information about a crime that has been committed |
| **heir** | someone who will legally receive another person's money, property, possessions or position when that person dies |
| **helmet** | a hard hat that protects the head against injury - a crash helmet must be worn by someone who is riding a motorcycle |

| | |
|---|---|
| **heroin** | a type of drug which is addictive, powerful and illegal (see addictive substance) |
| **higher education** | education that students receive at college or university |
| **holding public office** | having a job in one of the services or industries that are managed by the government |
| **Holy Land** | the area in the Middle East in and around Jerusalem where all the biblical events took place |
| **House of Commons** | that part of the Houses of Parliament where MPs who are elected by the voting public debate political issues |
| **House of Lords** | that part of the Houses of Parliament where the people who have inherited seats or been especially chosen by the Prime Minister debate political issues |
| **Houses of Parliament** | the building in London which comprises the House of Commons, the House of Lords and other offices where the British Parliament meets, debates and passes laws |
| **household** | the home and the people who live in it/something that relates to the home, e.g. household chores are jobs that need to be done in the home like cleaning and cooking |
| **humiliated** | feel ashamed, stupid or embarrassed because of something that happens to you, usually when other people are there |
| **immigration** | enter another country to live and work there - someone who does this is an immigrant (see migrate) |
| **inappropriate touching** | touching someone on a part of his/her body or in a way that is offensive and not acceptable in a particular situation |

**indecent remarks**     something that is said that contains words which are rude, sexual and offensive

**independents (politics)**     MPs who do not represent any of the main political parties

**inflation (money)**     the rate at which prices rise over a period of time

**infrastructure**     structured network that is necessary for the successful operation of a business or transport system, e.g. roads or railways

**inheritance**     a sum of money, possessions or property that someone has the legal right to receive after the death of (usually) a relative, e.g. a son might inherit his father's fortune

**inhuman (behaviour)**     very harsh, cruel and degrading

**innocent (law)**     found by a court NOT to be responsible for committing a crime (see guilty)

**inpatient**     someone who needs medical care and needs to stay in hospital overnight or longer

**instalments (money)**     a series of equal payments which are paid regularly over a period of time until the total cost of something is paid, e.g. a person may pay for a TV that costs £200 in ten monthly instalments of £20

**insulting words**     rude words which also make people feel very unhappy, worried or stupid

**insure**     pay money to an insurance company in case e.g. a car or property is damaged – if this happens, the insurance company will help to pay for repairs

**intentionally**     on purpose, deliberately

| | |
|---|---|
| **interest (money)** | extra money that must be paid to a lender when someone borrows money – this is usually calculated as a percentage of the loan. If the interest rate is 10% and the person borrows £100, the interest that must be paid on the loan will be an extra £10 |
| **internet café** | a place where people can go and pay to use a computer to look up information on websites or to send emails – the cost depends on how long they want to use a computer for, e.g. 30 minutes |
| **interpreter** | a person whose job is to change something that is spoken or written in one language into another language without changing the meaning |
| **irretrievably broken down** | when there is no hope of solving problems and making a bad situation better again |
| **Islamic mortgage** | a loan for buying a house, and when the person who receives the loan only needs to pay back the original sum – no extra money needs to be paid (see interest) |

| | |
|---|---|
| **judge (law)** | the most important official in court whose job is to make sure that court proceedings are lawful and fair, and to decide which punishment to give a criminal if s/he is found guilty by the court |
| **judiciary** | all the judges in a country who, together, are responsible for using the law of the land in the correct way |
| **jury** | ordinary people (usually a group of 12 people) who listen to information and then decide whether someone is guilty or innocent in a court of law |

**labour (employment)**  work which is often physical/workers

**landlord, landlady (housing)**  a man (landlord) or woman (landlady) who owns a house or flat and rents it to people (tenants) who must pay them money (rent) to live there

**landlord, landlady (pub)**  the owner or manager of a pub

**lane (transport)**  part of a road, usually marked by white lines, which is only wide enough for one vehicle to travel in (see carriageway)

**legal**  allowed to do by law or must do by law

**legal aid**  money that a person can ask for to help them pay for the services of a solicitor and, if necessary, court costs

**legal procedure**  the way that something is done by law

**legislative power**  the power to make laws

**legitimate children**  children whose parents are married to each other when they are born

**leisure centre**  a building where people can go and pay to do sports indoors, e.g. swimming, badminton

**letting agent**  a service which helps landlords find tenants and helps tenants find places to rent (see landlord, landlady)

**liberty**  freedom

**lock**  close something securely, usually with a key, so that other people cannot easily open it

| | |
|---|---|
| **long-standing** | having already existed for a long time |
| **L-plates** | a sign on a car to show that the driver is still learning to drive and has not yet passed their driving test - an L-plate is a red 'L' in a white square |

| | |
|---|---|
| **magistrate** | a person who acts as a judge in a court case where the crime is not as serious as some others |
| **mainland** | an area of land which forms a country and does not include any of its surrounding islands |
| **manufacturer** | the maker of a product which is sold to the public |
| **marital status** | information about whether a person is single, married, separated or divorced that is often asked for on official forms |
| **maternity leave** | time allowed off work for a woman during her pregnancy and after her baby is born and during which time she usually continues to receive a wage (see paternity leave) |
| **maternity services** | medical and social help relating to motherhood from early pregnancy until after the baby has been born |
| **media** | all the organisations that give information to the public, e.g. newspapers, magazines, television, radio and the internet |
| **mediation** | advice and support given by a person or organisation to end an argument between two other people or groups of people who cannot agree about something |
| **medical consultation** | speaking to a doctor and getting information and advice, e.g. about health issues, illness |

| | |
|---|---|
| **mental illness** | an illness in which a person appears to behave or think in ways that are not considered to be normal, e.g. 'depression' is a mental illness that makes people feel unnecessarily sad, worried or frightened and can prevent them from doing routine things like shopping, having fun with friends etc. |
| **meter (housing)** | a machine that shows, in units or numbers, how much electricity, gas or water has been used in a household |
| **meter reading (housing)** | the number on a meter that shows how much electricity, gas or water has been used |
| **migrate (people)** | move to another country to live and work there – someone who does this is a migrant (see immigration) |
| **military service, compulsory** | every adult (usually male) must join the armed forces for a particular period of time – this is not required by law in the UK |
| **minor offences** | illegal actions or activities that are considered NOT to be very serious, e.g. theft of a very small amount of money (see serious offences) |
| **mislead (law)** | give wrong or incomplete or false information on purpose so that someone else is not told the truth |
| **missionaries** | people who travel to other countries to teach and spread a religious faith |
| **misuse** | use something in a wrong way or for a wrong reason |
| **molestation** | a sexual attack on someone (often a child) |
| **monarch** | the king or queen of a country |

| | |
|---|---|
| **monopoly (business)** | a power which has exclusive control over a supply of goods or over a service and where competitors are not allowed to deal in the same business |
| **mortgage** | a loan, usually from a building society or bank, that is used to buy or help buy a house or flat – the loan is usually paid back in instalments over a number of years (see building society) |
| **motor (transport)** | a machine that makes something move/a car |
| **MP** | Member of Parliament – the person who is elected by his or her constituents to represent them in government |

| | |
|---|---|
| **national issues** | political problems that can affect everyone who lives in a country |
| **nationalised** | bought and then controlled by central government – relating to an industry or service that was previously owned privately (see privatise) |
| **naturalised citizen** | someone who is born in one country but becomes a citizen of another country |
| **nobility** | the group of people in a country who belong to the highest social class – some of whom may have titles, e.g. Lord or Duke (see aristocracy) |
| **not-for-profit** | a way of doing business in which an organisation or company will not try to make any money from providing their service or goods |
| **notice, to give** | to give someone information about something that is going to happen in the future that will change a situation |

| | |
|---|---|
| **notice (employment)** | a length of time that an employee must continue to work after telling an employer that s/he wants to leave the job/a length of time that an employer must continue to employ someone after asking her/him to leave, e.g. my boss only gave me one week's notice so I was really upset |
| **nuisance (behaviour)** | something that annoys or causes problems for other people |
| **obstructive (behaviour)** | being difficult, and stopping someone from doing something or stopping something from happening on purpose |
| **occupy a country** | invade a country and take control of it |
| **occupation (employment)** | job |
| **offensive (behaviour)** | rude and upsetting |
| **office, to be in** | to be in power in government |
| **off-licence** | a shop that sells alcohol in bottles or cans, e.g. wine, beer |
| **Olympic team** | a team of sportsmen and women who represent their country in the Olympics - an international athletics competition held every four years |
| **online** | on the internet |
| **on-the-spot fines** | an immediate demand for money which must be paid as a punishment for doing something wrong, e.g. to receive an on-the-spot fine for driving too fast |

**Opposition**     the second largest party that is not in power in the government, e.g. in 2006, the Labour Party was in power and the Conservatives were in Opposition and David Cameron was the Leader of the Opposition

**outpatient**     someone who needs medical care in a hospital but does not need to stay overnight

**packaging**     material, e.g. boxes, see-through plastic, that covers and protects things that are for sale, e.g. food

**padlock**     a small lock which can be used to keep things safe and secure by stopping anyone else opening or stealing them

**party politics**     the shared and particular ideas and beliefs of an organised group of politicians, e.g. the Labour Party

**paternity leave**     time allowed off work for a man whose wife or partner is going to have a baby or has just had a baby and during which time he usually continues to receive a wage (see **maternity leave**)

**patient (medical)**     someone whom a doctor looks after or who needs medical care because they are ill, have an injury etc.

**patriarchy**     a system of society in which men hold all the power and in which power can be passed from father to son

**patriotism**     the pride of belonging to, and love of, a country

**patron saint**     a Christian saint who, according to religious belief, protects a particular place or a particular group of people

**peers**  members of the House of Lords

**penalty (law)**  punishment for breaking the law, e.g. a fine (see on-the-spot fines)

**pension plan, pay into a**  to save money regularly while a person is working so that when a person stops going to work at 60 or older, there will be enough money to provide him/her with a pension (see State Pension)

**performing (theatre)**  acting or dancing

**perishable food**  food which can go bad and become uneatable quite quickly, e.g. fresh meat and fish, milk

**permit (law)**  a document that allows someone to legally do something, e.g. a work permit

**persecuted**  hunted and punished, perhaps even killed, e.g. someone might be persecuted for holding a particular religious belief

**personal details**  information about a person that can be used to identify them, e.g. their name, date of birth, address, marital status etc.

**personnel officer**  someone whose job in a company is to employ staff and to help solve problems that employees have at work

**phonecard, pre-paid**  a card that can be bought and then used to make a certain number of phone calls up to the value of the card

| | |
|---|---|
| **PIN number** | four numbers which have to be tapped into a cash machine if someone wants to withdraw money from their account or pay for something using credit or debit cards. Using a personal identification number (PIN) stops other people from using cards if they are stolen so the numbers must be remembered and kept secret |
| **places of worship** | religious buildings like churches or mosques where people can go to practise their religion, e.g. to pray or sing |
| **plague (medical)** | a disease that people easily catch from one another and from which many people die at a particular time in history |
| **pluralistic society** | a society in which the population is multi-racial, multi-religious and has many different political ideas |
| **pocket money** | a small amount of money that a parent might give to his/her child on a regular basis, e.g. once a week, so that the child can buy his/her own comics or sweets etc. |
| **pogroms** | the intentional killing of many people usually because of their race or religious belief |
| **pooled savings** | amounts of money that have been saved by different people and added together to make a larger sum of jointly-owned money |
| **Pope, the** | the leader of the Roman Catholic Church |
| **possessions** | things that people own, e.g. a car, clothes, a television, books |
| **practise a religion** | actively live according to the rules, customs and beliefs of that religion, e.g. go to church, take part in prayer, wear special clothing etc. |

**pregnancy**    the nine-month period before birth during which a baby grows inside its mother - the mother is pregnant at this time

**prehistoric**    a time in history before any records were written down

**prescription (medical)**    a note from a doctor saying which medicines a patient needs

**pressure group**    a group of people who try to persuade the government to do something or to persuade the public to change their opinion about something

**Prime Minister**    the Member of Parliament who is the leader of the political party in power and therefore of the whole government

**privatised**    bought and then controlled by the private sector - relating to an industry or service that was previously owned by the government (see nationalised)

**process of precedent**    a system in which previous actions or decisions influence and support future actions or decisions (often in legal judgements)

**prohibit**    say that something is illegal/stop someone doing something/make something illegal or forbid something

**promotion (employment)**    movement to a better or to a more important job within the same company, e.g. she was promoted from shop assistant to sales manageress

**proof**    information, items, documents etc. that show that something has definitely happened (see evidence)

| | |
|---|---|
| **proportional representation** | a system of election in which political parties are allowed a number of seats in Parliament that represents their share of the total number of votes cast |
| **prosperity** | a time of wealth or increase in fortune |
| **provinces** | areas into which a country is divided for governmental reasons |
| **pub** | public house - a place where adults over the age of 18 can buy and drink alcohol |
| **public, a member of the** | an person who is an ordinary member of the community and not a government official |
| **public body** | a governmental department or a group of people who represent or work for the government and work for the good of the general public |
| **public order (law)** | a situation where rules are obeyed in a public place |
| **public place** | a place which is not private and where ordinary people can spend time together, or on their own, e.g. a cinema, a restaurant, a library, a pub, a park |
| **punctual** | arriving at the right time, not being late for something, e.g. work or a doctor's appointment |

| | |
|---|---|
| **racial** | relating to race, e.g. racial discrimination (see discrimination) |
| **racially-motivated crime** | a crime that is committed against someone because of their race or ethnic origin |
| **racism** | aggressive behaviour towards (or treatment of) people who come from a different race by people who wish to be unkind and unfair to them |

| | |
|---|---|
| **raising (family)** | looking after children as they grow so that they are safe and healthy |
| **rape** | the criminal act of a person forcing another person to have sex, often involving violence |
| **receipt (money)** | a piece of paper with a description of something that has been bought and its price – given by a shop to a customer as a record of the purchase |
| **recruit (employment)** | find people and offer them work in a company or business |
| **recycle rubbish** | separate rubbish into different materials, e.g. put all the paper in one place and all the glass in another, so that each material can be processed in a separate way and used again, e.g. broken glass can be made into new bottles |
| **redundant (employment)** | no longer needed to do a particular job, e.g. if a person is made redundant, there is no longer a job for that person to do in a particular company and they will be asked to leave – if this happens the employee may be entitled to receive an amount of money (redundancy pay) |
| **referendum** | a vote by the public or by a governing body to decide on a course of action or to make a political decision |
| **Reformation, the** | the religious movement in the 16th century that challenged the authority of the Pope and established Protestant churches in Europe – Protestant comes from the word 'protest' |
| **refuge** | a place where a person can stay and be kept safe from danger |
| **refugees** | people who must leave the country where they live, often because of war or political reasons (see asylum seekers) |

| | |
|---|---|
| **refund (money)** | give a customer an amount of money back that is equal to the price of something s/he bought but returned to the shop, e.g. because the item does not work properly |
| **remain silent (police)** | say nothing, not to answer questions |
| **rent (housing)** | pay to live in a room, flat or house that is owned by someone else |
| **report a crime** | tell the police about an illegal action or activity |
| **residence** | the place where someone lives, their address |
| **residential trips (school)** | visits to places when students stay away from home for one night or longer and have to sleep in other accommodation |
| **resign (employment)** | decide officially to leave a certain job |
| **restrict (immigration)** | control and/or limit the number of people, e.g. a government might restrict the number of immigrants who can come and live in a country |
| **retail work** | jobs that involve working in shops and selling goods to customers |
| **retire (employment)** | stop going to work, usually at the age of 65 or older |
| **rise (in number, price)** | increase, go up |
| **rival viewpoints** | opinions that are held by different people or groups of people that are in opposition to each other |

| | |
|---|---|
| **roots (family)** | the place that someone relates to because that was where s/he was born or where his/her family had their established home |
| **scratch card** | a card that a person buys and then rubs with a coin to see if they have won money (see gambling) |
| **scrutinise** | examine all the details |
| **seat (government)** | a position that is officially held by someone in government who has been elected by the public and authorised to represent them |
| **second-hand goods** | something that someone else has already owned |
| **security** | protection from something that could be dangerous, e.g. a person or thing that is secure is safe and protected from danger |
| **self-employed person** | someone who works for themselves and not for an employer |
| **sentence (law)** | length of time a criminal must stay in prison as a punishment for the crime s/he has committed-this is decided by a judge at the end of a court case |
| **separation (family)** | a situation where a married couple no longer live together but are not yet divorced |
| **serious misconduct (employment)** | behaviour by someone in a job which is dishonest, bad or unprofessional, and because of which they may lose their job |
| **serious offences (law)** | illegal actions or activities which are very bad and for which someone may have to go to prison for a long time, e.g. rape, murder (see minor offences) |

**Shadow Cabinet**  a group of senior MPs with special responsibilities who belong to a party that is not in government (which can also be called the Opposition)

**Sheriff (law)**  a judge in Scotland

**sick pay**  money received by an employee when s/he is unable to work because of illness

**signatory**  a person who signs their name (puts their signature) on an official document - e.g. to show their agreement to an official arrangement

**slavery**  a system in which people bought and owned other people (slaves) who were then forced to work for nothing in return (see forced labour)

**solicitor**  a professional person whose job is to give legal advice and prepare documents for legal procedures, e.g. divorce, buying and selling houses

**Speaker, the**  the person in government who controls the way issues are debated in Parliament

**stand for office**  apply to be elected as an MP or local councillor

**standing order**  an arrangement in which a bank or building society takes a fixed amount of money from one account and pays it into another account on a regular basis (see direct debit)

**start-up loans**  money given to someone to start up a new business that must be paid back with interest later (see grant, interest)

**State Pension**  money paid regularly by the government to people who have retired from work, usually when they are 65 or older

**stepfamily**  a family in which the mother or father is not the biological parent of one or more of the children, e.g. when a divorced woman re-marries, her new husband will be the stepfather to the children from her previous marriage

**strike, to go on**  refuse to work in order to protest against something, e.g. low wages, long hours

**subscribe to a magazine**  pay enough money so that copies of a magazine can be sent to an address at regular intervals over a period of time (usually for a year)

**successor (government)**  a person who comes after another and who will often receive some kind of power when that happens, e.g. a son who becomes king when his father, the old king, dies is the successor to the throne

**surveyor (housing)**  a person who examines a property (usually when it is for sale) and checks the condition of the building. S/he then writes an official report (a survey) which gives important information to the buyer about any problems, or about any repairs that might need to be done

**suspect (crime)**  a person who police think may be guilty of a committing a crime, but this is not certain yet

**suspend**  to officially stop, usually for a short time, something from happening or operating

**taster session (training)**  an introductory part of a course that allows someone to try it and to see if it is what they would like to do

**tenancy**  the period of time that a tenant rents a property from a landlord or landlady - often also relating to conditions about renting the property

**tenant** — a person who pays money to a landlord to live in rented accommodation - a flat or a house

**terrorism** — violence used by people who want to force governments to do something-the violence is usually random and unexpected so no one can feel really safe from it

**theft** — the criminal act of stealing something from a person, building or place (see burglary)

**therapist (psychology)** — a professional person whose job is to help people to understand why they have problems and to help them solve their problems

**timescale** — the planned length of time it takes to complete something, usually at work

**toddler (family)** — small child, usually 1-2 years old - the age at which small children learn to walk

**torture** — hurt someone in a very cruel way and on purpose, e.g. to try to make them give information or to punish them

**tow away a car** — remove a car from a place - another vehicle pulls it along - usually because it has been illegally parked

**trade union** — an association of workers that protects its members' political rights

**trader** — someone who trades - who buys and sells goods

**treaty** — an official written agreement between countries or governments

**tried in front of a judge** — facts of the case heard and the sentence decided in an official court of law

**tuition fees** — money paid to a teacher or to a school for being taught something

| | |
|---|---|
| **unemployed** | not doing a job and not getting any wages |
| **uprising** | a violent revolt or rebellion against an authority |
| **utilities, public** | services that the public can use, e.g. the supply of water, gas or electricity |

| | |
|---|---|
| **vacancy (employment)** | a job that is available and that an employer needs someone to do |
| **valid** | legally acceptable, e.g. when someone wants to enter another country his/her passport must be valid for that to be allowed |
| **vehicle (transport)** | something in which people can travel on the roads, e.g. a car or bus |
| **vetoed, to be vetoed** | officially refused permission to do something, often by an organisation |
| **victim** | someone who is hurt or harmed by something that another person has done |
| **vocational course** | a series of lessons in which a student is taught the practical skills that are necessary to do a certain job, e.g. to become a plumber or car mechanic (see academic course) |
| **volt** | a measurement of electrical force |
| **voluntarily** | in a willing way, e.g. a person who does something voluntarily does it because they want to, and not because someone has asked them to do it or because someone has said that they must do it |
| **voluntary work** | work which someone does because they want to and which they do for free, i.e. they do not receive any payment (see volunteer) |

| | |
|---|---|
| **volunteer** | someone who works for free or who offers to do something without payment (see voluntary work) |
| **vulnerable people** | people who can be easily hurt or harmed e.g. because of their age |

| | |
|---|---|
| **wages (pay)** | an amount of money paid for work |
| **war effort** | the work that people did in order to support the country in whatever way they could during wartime |
| **welfare benefits** | amounts of money paid by the government to people who have very little money of their own and who are perhaps unable to work or elderly or sick or disabled etc. |
| **will (law)** | a legal document that gives instructions about what a person wants to happen when s/he dies, e.g. about who should have their property, money or possessions |
| **withdraw (law)** | step back from and stop taking part in a formal arrangement or activity |
| **withdraw (money)** | take money out of a bank account or cash machine |
| **workforce** | the group of people who work for a particular company or business or, on a larger scale, all the people who can work in a particular country or part of the world etc. |
| **working days** | the days on which, typically, most people go to work – in the UK these are Monday, Tuesday, Wednesday, Thursday and Friday |

| | |
|---|---|
| **Yellow Pages** | a book that lists names, addresses and telephone numbers of businesses, services and organisations in an area |

Copies of this publication can be made available in
alternative formats.

Standard (small print) version ISBN 978-0-11-341313-3
Audio/CD version ISBN 978-0-11-341318-8
These can be ordered from www.tsoshop.co.uk